Rosa Nouchette Carey

**Wooed and married**

Vol. III

Rosa Nouchette Carey

**Wooed and married**
*Vol. III*

ISBN/EAN: 9783337040833

Printed in Europe, USA, Canada, Australia, Japan

Cover: Foto ©ninafisch / pixelio.de

More available books at **www.hansebooks.com**

# WOOED AND MARRIED.

## A Novel.

---

BY

ROSA NOUCHETTE CAREY,

AUTHOR OF
"NELLIE'S MEMORIES," "WEE WIFIE," "BARBARA HEATHCOTE'S TRIAL,"
AND "ROBERT ORD'S ATONEMENT."

IN THREE VOLUMES.

VOL. III.

LONDON:
TINSLEY BROTHERS, 8, CATHERINE STREET, STRAND.
1875.

*[Right of Translation reserved by the Author.]*

# CONTENTS

OF

## THE THIRD VOLUME.

| CHAP. | | PAGE |
|---|---|---|
| I. | A FRAGMENT OF THE OLD, OLD STORY | 1 |
| II. | "IN THE MIDST OF LIFE" | 21 |
| III. | THROUGH THE CROSS TO THE CROWN | 41 |
| IV. | "QUI PATITUR VINCIT" | 67 |
| V. | "SOME DAYS MUST BE DARK AND DREARY" | 92 |
| VI. | "ALL IN THE WILD MARCH MORNING" | 117 |
| VII. | LITTLE FLORENCE | 136 |
| VIII. | AT BAY | 157 |
| IX. | DARKEST BEFORE DAWN | 176 |
| X. | CRUEL AS THE GRAVE | 198 |
| XI. | A SHADOW ON THE WALL | 219 |
| XII. | THE LAST OF THE COBWEBS | 238 |

# WOOED AND MARRIED.

## CHAPTER I.

### A FRAGMENT OF THE OLD, OLD STORY.

DYM was not without courage. The day after the wedding she set herself to take up her old duties again with a tolerable amount of determination and steadiness. It was dull; but life was dull, she said to herself, with a stoical shrug of the shoulders. She knew what Ingleside without Mr. Chichester was; and though she sorely and persistently missed him every hour of the day, she resolutely banished all painful regrets, and bore herself at least with outward cheerfulness.

Perhaps Humphrey's unselfishness had taught her something; but it was certain Mr. Chichester's last words had sunk deeply into her heart. "I leave you a precious legacy," he had said to her, with one of his winning smiles; and from that moment there was something sacred to Dym in the trust reposed in her. She would prove herself worthy of it; she would show him that hers was no hireling labour; if possible she would redouble her loving services to his mother, content if, on his return, he would reward her with one of his approving looks.

Guy Chichester had acted wisely in commending his mother to Dym's care. Dym had always been willing and affectionate, but her work had lacked enthusiasm; Guy's words had lent impetus to it. Mrs. Chichester soon felt the change in her young companion. Dym never complained of weariness now; she read, and wrote, and stitched, with laborious zeal; she sang little Scotch ballads in the evening, or drew her low chair to Mrs. Chichester's side, and beguiled a tedious hour by listening to stories of her friend's girlhood; she read Guy's and Honor's letters aloud over and over again, and kissed away the tears that sometimes stole down the mother's cheeks when any of their expressions of affection moved her more deeply than usual:

Now and then her old restless fits would return, but she never spoke of them; when the oppression became too great she would quietly steal out of the room, and muffling herself in her old plaid shawl, go out into the garden and shrubberies with Kiddle-a-wink. Dym had begged hard that Kiddle-a-wink might be left with her, and Humphrey had willingly agreed.

"Are you not afraid of taking cold? these spring evenings are very treacherous," Mrs. Chichester said to her once, when the girl came in, fresh and bright, to take up her work again.

"Oh, no; Kiddle-a-wink and I have had such a run," answered Dym, "down to the church porch and back again, and we met Mr. Nethecote."

Dym was always meeting Mr. Nethecote. Humphrey seemed to know intuitively the time for her rambles.

Mrs. Chichester smiled to herself, but she made no observation.

Dym seized every leisure moment for going over to Woodside; there were always two or three afternoons in the week when Mrs. Chichester did not need her; and she began regularly to go over for an hour or two, and give Rupert and Edgar their Latin lessons.

The work was partly pleasure; but she had an odd feeling growing on her of late that it was better for her to be employed. A few verses by Carlyle she had read in some book haunted her, and she was ever repeating them:

> So here has been dawning
> Another blue day;
> Think, wilt thou let it
> Slip useless away?
> Out of eternity
> This new day is born;
> Into eternity
> At night will return.

"This 'blue day' will bring nothing to me, but it may to others," she got into the habit of saying when she woke in the morning. Many people would have thought it a beautiful life: plenty of books, plenty of sunshine, a little work, piles of clever letters to read and answer, the great garden bloomimg with roses and lilies, the sleek horses coming round every day at the same hour, the luxurious equipage, the dainty five-o'clock tea, Dorothy coming in to warn her mistress it was time to dress, the quiet dinner, the brilliantly-lighted drawing-room. "Now read Guy's letter over again, my dear." Mrs. Chichester would kiss the thin foreign paper, with the well-known characters traced on it; but she was growing more blind every day. It would not be too much to say that she and Dym lived in those letters; Dym could almost hear Mr. Chichester's voice as she read those racy descriptions.

What wonderful glimpses they opened to her of continental life! Sometimes it was an old Belgian town, with grand churches and grass-grown streets, where they lingered for a day or two; now it was the blue Rhine, or some great city on the banks of the Danube. With the advanced summer Guy meant to make a detour into Switzerland, and so into the Italian Tyrol; there their wanderings must cease, Guy said, with some expressions of regret; for much as Honor wished to see Rome, she thought they ought to be home early in October. "Five months; it is a long time," sighed Mrs. Chichester; "but Guy was so bent on showing her all those places. How happy they seem, my dear! Now let us read Honor's." Honor's were always shorter than Guy's; but they were beautiful womanly letters; a sort of light seemed to reflect from them as Dym read—the pure radiance of a love that felt itself satisfied. Guy was evidently perfect in her eyes: Guy had taken such lovely old rooms, with a wooden balcony, looking over the river. Guy had stopped a day longer, because one day she had been tired, and she had missed the picture-gallery. In every few lines it was, "My wife;" "My husband." "All the artists are raving about my wife's beauty," wrote Guy. "One fellow, with a big yellow beard, has been praying me, with tears in his eyes, to let him paint her; he wants her for a 'Beatrice,' I believe; I suppose I must let him do it. If he manages to make a good thing of it I shall buy the picture myself. Fancy Honor, in a quaint green-velvet dress, 'and her hair studded with stars.'" "You must take this letter to Humphrey, he will like to see it," said Mrs. Chichester, as Dym folded it up; "you will be sure to see him to-morrow, when you go over to Woodside."

Dym checked a refractory speech that was rising to her lips. See him! was she not weary of seeing him? The fields between Ingleside and Nidderdale Cottage were haunted by this big burly figure with the broad-brimmed hat. Dym would have escaped him over and over again, but for Kiddle-a-wink, who never failed to greet his friend with a loud bark. Humphrey caught Dym once trying to scale a hedge, only her white dress gleamed through and betrayed her.

"Were you trying to run away from me?" asked Humphrey, with his sad kind smile; but Dym was confused, and would not answer him.

She hung down her head and walked by his side, and never once contradicted him. Humphrey certainly had the best of it that afternoon.

I wonder what Dym would have done if any one had told her Humphrey Nethecote was to be her fate—whether she would have called out loudly against the injustice, the impossibility of it, and have resigned herself to it after all? Many young creatures have had to put up with rough protectors, without a tithe of Humphrey's goodness, and have ended by becoming devoted wives. What was there about Dym that made this so impossible to her—that caused her to bridle and flush up at the least approach to tenderness on Humphrey's part, and to invest her sweetness with a hundred thorny prickles?

Mrs. Chichester's request was tantamount to a command, and there was therefore no reluctance in Dym's manner the next day, when she saw Humphrey coming down the road to meet her; on the contrary, she hastened her own footsteps.

But as she came up to him, after the first few minutes, her uneasiness returned. What was there about the fashion of the man that looked so altered? Humphrey was in the habit of wearing an old grey suit and leathern gaiters; the straw hat would be the worse for age, and brown with the sun: to-day his clothes were new, and fitted him; he had a white waistcoat and dark felt hat, and a jaunty little rose in his button-hole; he looked less angular; the old rusty air had left him; he looked what he was, a gentleman farmer in good condition. His honest freckled face had quite a bashful glow on it as he came up with Dym.

"I hardly knew you," said Dym dryly, as she handed him the letter. The new clothes, the rose, the picturesque slouched hat—what did it mean?

"I will read it presently," returned Humphrey, putting it in his pocket. "Mrs. Chichester shall have it back this evening."

"It will not take long. I would rather take it back," replied Dym, with a touch of her old contradiction. It was bad enough to have him the companion of all her walks, without his coming up to spoil their evening. Dym was turning decidedly restive.

"When do they come home, eh?" he asked, wrinkling his light eyebrows at her, but putting the letter safely in his pocket all the same. Dym had not yet found out Humphrey could be obstinate too.

"Not for six weeks. Let me see; it is August now—the summer seems as though it will never end," exclaimed Dym fractiously, as she shook out the folds of her light muslin dress, and with a discontented air smelt the roses Humphrey had brought her.

Humphrey was always bringing her roses—great bunches of delicious creamy roses, with a background of fern and heliotrope. As she scented their fragrance, she suddenly remembered sitting in the long narrow schoolroom at Lansdowne House, and Edith coming in and heaping her lap with these same roses.

Humphrey looked a little anxious over the girl's discontent and abrupt answers.

"When they come back you will have to go away," he said, with a touch of sorrow in his voice, which somehow moved her in spite of her humour.

Yes, she will have to go away, she tells him sadly enough now. There is no room for her then at Ingleside. Honor will take her place and work; no one will want her—no one—no one. The tears start to the girl's eyes as Humphrey takes her hand and makes her sit down on the little bench beside him.

Oddly enough, it is the very bench where Honor and Guy sat that May afternoon. It is August now; the gorse is as yellow as ever, but the heather is out, and the common is full of tender violet-bloom. The geese come up waddling as usual, stretching out their long white necks and yellow bills; up in the sky a lark is singing near a little white cloud.

"My dear," says Humphrey, with a break in his manly voice, for Dym's words are very pathetic, "somebody wants you—I want you."

Dym draws her hand away, a little startled.

"You are very good," she answers with an effort. "I don't deserve it." She is conscious that her words are tame—that she has hardly answered him; but what did he mean by saying that he wanted her?

"Don't go away from me," says Humphrey humbly, for in her odd confusion she is moving as far away as the bench will allow. "I have been wishing to speak to you all these months, and have never been able to summon up the courage. I want to tell you that you need not go away."

"I must go," returned Dym hurriedly. She was getting quite nervous now. Somehow her old friend was changed in his aspect this afternoon. It was not this sort of grave serious Humphrey she had teased. "I must go; there is no room for me at Ingleside. You do not know what you are talking about:" she went on trying to pluck up a little spirit with which to answer him, but it was a miserable failure.

"Yes, I do," replied Humphrey quite gravely, but speaking as gently as though to an infant, for he had no wish to frighten her. "But there are other houses besides Ingleside that will be glad to have you. I am all alone, Dym; why should you not come to me?"

"How—why—what do you mean?" she asked breathlessly; even now she does not understand him, and why—how dare he call her Dym?

"There is only one way in which you can come to me, dear. May I tell you what that is?"

But Dym jumps up from the seat and covers her face with her hands: her cheeks are burning now.

"No, no! Mr. Nethecote, why do you frighten me so? why are you so unlike yourself? You must not call me that. Oh, I am so unhappy!" But Dym was trembling, so that she was obliged to let him draw her again to her seat.

"Does it make you unhappy to know I love you?" asked Humphrey, mournfully. "It seems to me now that I have loved you ever since I raised my eyes and saw you peeping over the paper that day you came to Ingleside. I have gone on loving you every day since then, and it is not in my nature to leave off, I am afraid."

"Oh, please do!" Dym begged him. She was sobbing with agitation now. "It seems so dreadful, when I cannot—when you know I cannot—do it in return."

"Do what—love me?"

Dym nodded.

"I did not expect it—don't misunderstand me—how could you care much at first for such a rough fellow? But you say it makes you unhappy to go away. Will you"—his voice almost giving way with his earnestness—"won't you trust me? won't you let me take care of you? I would be content if you could only give me a very little, and let me love you."

"Please don't, Mr. Nethecote." The tears were fairly streaming down her face now. The good, generous Humphrey! "Oh, how sad, how dreadful it all seems! I like you so much that it makes it all the harder; but indeed I must go away."

"The Cottage is empty," he went on in his simple way. "I am almost a rich man now; Providence has been pleased to bless me. Do say you will come to me, dear; you don't half know how lonely it is, and how I am always thinking about you. There is not a hair of your head that is not dear to me—a man's love can be so strong."

But Dym only hid her face and cried.

"Will you not try to like me a little?" There was no help for it, he would have her answer.

Dym gave him a childish pitiful look as she put her hands down.

"Oh, I do like you very much, you are so good to me, Humphrey!" speaking his name for the first time. "I cannot bear to think that this has happened, and that you will cease to be my friend."

"My dear, I could not turn against you, whatever happens. I wish I could," he returned, with a faint smile. Poor Humphrey, how white his face had grown!

"And you will be my friend still?"

"Without doubt."

"Ah, how kind you are! I wish I could have done this, but it would not be right. I would not love you in that way. I am not what you think; I am foolish and vain. I should not have pleased you."

"You would have been good enough for me." How the big faithful heart was labouring with its pain! but not even now could he make pretty speeches. Good enough! Were not her words perfection? was she not pleasant to his eyes, the dearest, the sweetest? Something came up in Humphrey's throat and choked him as Dym made her honest little protest; she had spoken it in all good faith and humility. A few weeks ago she had been wondering if any one would love her; and now this man had come, and was almost overwhelming her with his tenderness. Oh, how good he was! Why could she not love him? How could she make him understand that she was thrilling with gratitude and sorrow, that his friendship was precious to her, and that she prayed never to lose it?

"Forgive me; do not be angry with me; I cannot help myself or you," she said, humbly stretching out her hand to him.

Humphrey pressed it gently, and laid it down. It would never be his—never—never!

"Why should I be angry? A woman's heart is not always to be won. I can't promise to give up loving you, Dym, but at least I will not trouble you with my sadness. By-and-bye, when I have got over this, it shall be as usual, and we will be friends."

"Yes, yes," she replied eagerly.

He had risen, and seemed waiting for her, and they walked silently on together. How Dym's head ached! how she longed to break the silence! to bid him leave her alone to her own thoughts; but she could not muster courage to address him.

Now and then she stole secret glances at the grave sad face; but Humphrey seemed lost in his sad thoughts. At the trysting-stile he suddenly stopped, and asked if she wished to go on alone.

Dym timidly answered "Yes."

"Then good-bye, dear. I am hardly myself just now, and perhaps it will be better. Try to forget about all this the next time we meet. I shall be your old friend Humphrey. Will you remember that?"

"And as Dym looked up in his face with sorrowful assent, he stooped down and kissed her brow as a brother might have done; and then, looking back with another kind smile, went striding home through the fields.

Dym had a very tender heart in spite of her faults, and it was nearly broken by Humphrey's last kind smile.

Mrs. Chichester wondered what ailed the girl that evening.

Dym was quite speechless and distraught.

After dinner, Mrs. Chichester beckoned her to take the low chair at her side; her fine woman's instinct guided her to subtle conclusions. Dym's voice had new startled tones in it; a little artful questioning, a few soothing caresses, and then it all came out.

Dym could not keep her pain to herself—she wanted to know if she had been very wicked; she put down her head on Mrs. Chichester's lap, as though she were a veritable child, and told her tale in agitated whispers. She had wounded the noblest heart—she should never be happy again. Humphrey loved her, and she could never be his wife—never—never!

"Is it very wicked of me?" cries poor Dym, laying her cheek against the kind hand; "one cannot make oneself love. I never thought of this, and I have often been so cross and ill-tempered with him, and he has borne with it all. Oh, what shall I do! I can never look him in the face again—never—I have made him so very, very unhappy."

Mrs. Chichester sighed, as she set herself to comfort the little culprit. Humphrey was an especial favourite, and she thought he deserved a better fate. She had set her heart on seeing Dym installed in Nidderdale Cottage; it would be so pleasant to keep her near them; and, to do her justice, she believed that Humphrey would make her an excellent husband.

It cost her something to relinquish her pet scheme. Under these circumstances perhaps it would be better for her *protégée* to leave Birstwith altogether. Humphrey would never be cured of his hopeless attachment while Dym remained at Ingleside. If only Dym was certain of her own mind! Mrs. Chichester was not quite so sure of it. She saw Dym was startled and repulsed by it now; but might she not bring herself to look upon it in a more sensible light? Humphrey's good qualities would make themselves felt after a time. These young girls require management and soothing, so Mrs. Chichester was not altogether sure of the hopelessness.

But Dym must be comforted at any cost, and she hastened to assure her that she had not been very wicked. These things were not always to be helped. On the whole she had behaved very well, and said all she ought to have said.

"We must leave it now; of course it is a great pity, and I am very grieved for poor Humphrey; but you must not make yourself ill with crying, my child; men have these troubles sometimes, and they always get over them. By-and-bye Humphrey and you will be the best of friends." But in this Mrs. Chichester lied to her own conviction; and Dym sorrowfully shook her head—she on her part did not think Humphrey would get over it.

Poor Humphrey! His honest heart would only have cleaved to her the more if he had known the grief with which the girl bewailed her own hardness of heart and his disappointment. To a true woman there can be nothing more sorrowful than to know that she has saddened some brave heart that has failed to win her love. The attachment may cause her some secret pride in the retrospect, but she will hardly boast of her conquests, as some of our modern Boadiceas do, when they count the captives they have dragged intentionally at their chariot-wheels, every one of whom had reason to hope he would be the victor.

I believe flirting is considered a very venial sin in most of our gay circles; the youth of one sex is considered to be proper prey for the other; to win admiration, to attract, to inveigle the unwary enemy by artful ambush and skilfully-planned sallies, is only held as lawful amusement. The queens of society acted more nobly in the ages of chivalry, when they sold their charms to the bravest bidder; women were as ready then to place themselves at their highest worth. It seems strange to us now to think of them smiling in scenes of horrid confusion and bloodshed—the fair lady of the tournament looking over the tapestried barrier with unshrinking eyes at shivering lances and riderless horses, and broken casques streaming with blood. She gives her slim hand and the golden chain together to the victor as he rides up; he is stained with dust and blood; his armour is hacked, and shows grisly wounds through the rents; the discomfited rivals limp off the field; it is to be hoped, however, she has no lurking preference for the one with yellow hair instead of black; if she has, she masks her anguish under smiles. She dresses her victorious lover's wounds with balm and ointment. Fancy any of our Belgravian ladies doing the same for their lovers! The tournament is over. Everything is fair in love and war. Doubtless the yellow-haired knight would have made a villanous caitiff of a husband. Up with the tents, and forward to the castle; victor and vanquished will feast merrily together in the great hall presently.

But Dym was no fashionable lady. Her heart had not yet been hardened and inflated by the triumphs of a season. She was unsophisticated enough to feel heartily sorry that all this had happened. Perhaps she was not so unhappy as Humphrey, after all—poor Humphrey, who sat knocking the ashes out of the pipe he has not smoked, and rating himself for a fool—a middle-aged fool—who had not learned yet that his heart ought to be growing grey with his head, that he should love soberly, and content himself with moderate wishes, and not think that he could place a fair young figure by his hearth who would be still young while he was old, whose tenderness was no fit mate for his roughness.

"Fool that I was ever to think she could fancy me," he groaned; "and worse than fool, to imagine that a young thing as she is could be tempted merely by an offer of a home. I wonder if she will ever find any one to love her as I do, or work for her either, soft-hearted blundering fellow as I am. She would not have needed to lift her little finger; I'd have made the Cottage such a bower she'd hardly have known it, if she would only have come to me. But if I loved her a hundred years, she would never care for me; no one but Katie ever did." And Humphrey looked round the empty room that no woman's presence was to brighten for him.

Humphrey was too humble and sweet-tempered to rail over his evil fortune. After a time he bore his trouble with his old stoical fortitude; good and ill had come to him, and he had accepted both with the same pious submission; it was not his way to complain. In his and Honor's veins there was a tinge of Scotch blood. His mother, Elspie Nethecote, was descended from the old Covenanters; among his ancestors were stern red-bearded Highlanders, who had fallen before the sword of Claverhouse, who were massacred in glens and wildernesses for adhering to the simple formulas of their national faith. In spite of his softheartedness and slow gentle ways, Humphrey at times proved himself worthy of the noble stock whence he had sprung. Life had taught endurance to both him and Honor. Though his heart was sore within him for many and many a long day, and his cheerless hearth became more cheerless, he would have scorned to be crushed under his misfortune. "Happy or unhappy, we must do our duty," was his and Honor's motto; and nobly did Humphrey fulfil his.

Early and late he worked as heretofore; there were fields to sow and harvests to reap, though the dark-eyed girl he loved would not come to him and make his home pleasant to him. Sometimes, as he looked round his richly-stocked garners, and saw himself adding acre to acre, and knew that he should die wifeless and childless, the sad thought would cross him, Of what good was it all, when none should come after him? True, Honor might have children, but they would not need his wealth. What should he do with the good things that came so freely at his bidding? And the answer seemed vague and distant enough.

Humphrey meant to keep his word when he promised Dym that he should remain her friend. It would have been simply impossible to have avoided her, even had such an intention ever formed itself in his mind; he must have come upon her again and again in church, in the village, in the fields that must be crossed and recrossed at morning and evening.

Dym went a long way round the road the next time she went to Woodside. She started and turned pale at every long shadow thrown over the sunny path. If she missed seeing Humphrey for the next few days, it was not because he intended to avoid her for his own sake—it was only his thoughtfulness that shielded her from a chance meeting till the wound had a little healed over, and he could say the ordinary friendly words that should set her at her ease. Humphrey argued stoutly with himself that it was all one whether he saw her or not; the pain would be a little harder to bear, perhaps, when her winsome face was actually before him; but in the long-run it would be all the same. Absence would not help him; time only could heal the wound that was for ever breaking out afresh. "By-and-bye, when I am old, the pain will die away," he thought; "when she is married, perhaps, and has children of her own, she will not be afraid of her old friend then." And then came into his simple mind a score of pleasant pictures, for all their background of sadness: how he would befriend her and them; how the one with the mother's eyes should be his favourite, and grow up upon his knee—should inherit the broad acres, perhaps, of Nidderdale Farm; he thought how proud he would be of them, and how he would be called Old Humphrey among them, and how she and her husband—" and whoever he might be, God bless him!"—thought Humphrey, should find in him the truest friend.

Ah! peace with thee, honest Humphrey; the dream goes on, and the aching sadness goes on, and fresh troubles cloud the horizon, and stormy days are in store for thee and all thou lovest! Oh, when the heavens are black with clouds and darkness, and one gallant vessel founders on the rocks, I can see thee bravely taking thy part, and battling with conflicting elements; and I know that the dream will come true, and that thy battered bark shall come into fair haven at last!

## CHAPTER II.

### "IN THE MIDST OF LIFE."

DYM turned quite white when she saw Humphrey next: he came into the drawing-room at Ingleside one evening when Dym was reading to Mrs. Chichester.

"I have brought the letter back," said Humphrey quietly. He does not stammer, or blunder over Mrs. Chichester's footstool in his usual luckless fashion. He shook hands with Dym very gravely as he noted the whiteness. If it had been in his power, he would have saved her this awkwardness. "Have you been quite well, Miss Elliott?" he asked presently, with his old kind smile. Humphrey was bearing himself quite bravely, while pale Dym was shrinking into her corner.

"We have had another letter since then," observed Mrs. Chichester with a sigh; she was very sorry for Humphrey, and Dym too, but her mind was full of other things. "I have had a great disappointment, Humphrey, but—but you must read it for yourself."

"They are not coming home," Humphrey argues shrewdly, as he unfolds the letter; it is written from Salzburg, and is in Guy's handwriting, but, as usual, there is a little note from Honor.

Guy's letters had always been perfect in his mother's eyes, but this one was unusually loving, as though the writer wished to soften some great disappointment he felt he must inflict: "My dearest mother knows we are longing to see her," he wrote, "and that no consideration but one could induce us to defer our return. Honor was dreaming of Ingleside last night; she is always talking of our home and you, and what we are to do when we are together again; we have both decided there is nothing like Old England after all; and I am afraid Honor is just a trifle home sick"—a "For shame, Guy, with you!" scored under, in Honor's large firm handwriting.—"But, darling mother, there is a 'but' to all this. Dr. Guthrie (you may know his name in the London *Directory*) is staying at our hotel here. Honor has been ailing with a cold lately, and I thought it best to consult him. He gave us his opinion, which coincides exactly with Dr. Grey's—by-the-bye, he speaks very highly of him; they were friends and fellow students in the 'auld lang syne'—they both say Honor's chest was weakened by that illness of hers, and that an English winter would be very trying to her; however, he recommends us, by all means, to do Rome and Venice *en passant*, and then to winter either at Nice or Mentone. I can assure you, dearest mother, we both looked very grave over this advice. There can be no doubt as to what we ought to do; but it goes so hard with both of us to disappoint you; we had set our hearts on spending Christmas at Ingleside. You will be so dull without your children; and then there is the chance of that operation in February. If we do this, you will not see us till we have celebrated the anniversary of our wedding; for I could not bring my wife home till I knew the cold spring winds had died out of our valley." Honor's letter, too, was full of anxious tenderness; the wife's heart was evidently yearning for her husband's home, and the loving duties that awaited her.

"I think this has come to teach us that our happiness is almost too perfect," wrote Honor; "it does us good to have our wishes crossed just now, if only you were not to be included in our disappointment. Guy sighs, and says, 'Poor mother,' and then scolds me because I echo the sigh; he will have it I am home sick, because I dream so often of dear beautiful Ingleside. But is it not my home? Keep our places warm for us, mother; I wish I could put my arms round you, and kiss away the tears which I feel will come when you read our letters, and know Guy is not coming back to you yet. Guy sends his love to Dym; tell her we shall both love her better for taking such care of you."

Poor Mrs. Chichester looks at Humphrey for comfort as he reads both letters slowly. "Christmas without them; and I was beginning to get their rooms ready." She sighs, and another heavy wrinkle crosses Humphrey's brow. As he sits there, under the lamplight, Dym can see the light frizzy hair is streaked with grey, and so are the rough whiskers and beard; Dym wonders she has never noticed it before. She reddens as Humphrey raises his eyes and sees her looking at him; and Humphrey draws his hand nervously across his mouth. "It is best as it is," he says, with a blunt attempt at consolation; "the Duchess's chest has not been too strong, of late years, and when two doctors agree we have a chance of getting at the truth. Depend upon it the Squire's right, and it is no good fretting ourselves over what can't be helped." Humphrey's voice was a little husky over his philosophy. Mrs. Chichester shook her head as she detected it.

"You always speak cheerfully, Humphrey; but you know the winter will be long to you as well as to me."

"Madam will have her say," replies poor Humphrey, with a smile at Dym; but somehow Dym is not ready for it, and meets it very gravely. She breathes more freely when Humphrey gives her his hand and goes away. She shuts herself up in her room for a long time afterwards, but Mrs. Chichester wisely forbears all inquiries. Dym cannot look at her friend yet without sorrow; his grey hairs, the coldness of his hand, and those slow gentle smiles of his, are continually before her. Nothing comforted her so much as a long letter from Will, when he heard of her trouble. Will said nothing about his disappointment at the news; he did not even reproach her with her strange blindness, or say a single word as to Humphrey's virtues. He saw the girl's tender heart was bruised by the pain she had inflicted, and, like Mrs. Chichester, he strove to comfort.

"Be always my honest tender-hearted Dym, and tell me all that troubles you," he wrote. "I liked your letter, dear; it made me feel proud of my sister as I read it. I think it is noble and really womanly to feel as you are feeling; I would not spare you one tear that refusal has cost you. I would not have my child a whit less humble and child-like. All is as it should be; now you must try to forget it. Put away from you every thought, except that you have a very good and faithful friend. I do not like that expression, 'When I think of Humphrey I feel as though I should never be happy again.' My dear, the good God never meant us to bear other people's burdens in that way. Leave Nethecote to do his part, and battle through his disappointment; and remember it is a real duty now as heretofore to 'cultivate cheerfulness.'"

Dym used to read out bits of Will's letters to Mrs. Chichester. Mrs. Chichester used to say they were as fine as some of St. Francis de Sales'. Both women had lately elevated the pious Bishop of Geneva to be their favourite saint. "He is so cheerful, my dear," Mrs. Chichester would say. Poor lady! what with her blindness and the long lonely winter that was approaching, she had much ado to preserve her cheerfulness, especially as she had such an unreasonable dread of the operation which every day became more inevitable.

The mischief had been slowly working for years. It was wonderful how long she had contrived to deceive her son. Dorothy used to read to her mistress before Miss Elliott came. Dym's refined voice and clear modulations were a perfect treat after Dorothy's high-pitched rasping tones. Most of the household were conversant with their mistress's misfortune long before it became a subject of conversation at the Vicarage. "You know now why Miss Elliott came," observed the Vicar, a little reprovingly. Katherine shrugged her shoulders; it was a habit of hers to find fault with most of aunt Constance's sayings and doings. "I call it flying in the face of Providence, going about alone as she does," she replied severely. "She actually wanted me not to send Kenneth up to the house with her the other afternoon—was sure she could find her way alone; and when I asked where Miss Elliott was, I found she was over at Woodside, as usual, teaching those boys; as though Guy gives her a hundred a year to teach Rupert Grey Latin. I call it downright robbery and neglect," finished that lady in her most virtuous tones.

"I don't think you ever will approve of works of supererogation, Kitty," returned her husband sleepily; "if any one but Miss Elliott had done it we should have heard a different version. How you two women hate each other!" and the Vicar lounged off to his study and his sermon, thinking what a pity it was Katherine had such strong prejudices, and had taken such a dislike to that nice pretty Miss Elliott.

In November Mrs. Chichester took Dym up to London with her; and they stayed for a long time at Lansdowne House. Dym sat in the long narrow schoolroom again, and made friends with Mrs. Vivian's successor, and once, by special favour, spent an hour alone in her old garret. Anna Freiligrath, the young German governess, found her curled up there among her boxes, and staring with dim eyes over the strip of grey sky and the tall white shining roofs, behind which a dull red sun was sinking..

"*Ach himmel, liebe freunde*, thou wilt be starved with cold," cried the warm-hearted Anna, as she rubbed Dym's blue little hands. She was an honest, good-natured girl, and was always ready to *tutoyer* and otherwise pet Miss Elliott.

Dym struck up an alliance with the sturdy little German. Anna's flaxen plaits, her round blue eyes, her pale freckled face, were a great contrast to Dym's dark eyes and graceful little figure. Anna's voluble tones, a little guttural; the grey stocking, bristling with needles, always produced from her pocket; her long stories about her brothers Albrecht and Rudolph in the Prussian army; and her anxiety that Dym should know they were Von Freiligrath, were highly amusing to Dym. When Mrs. Chichester could spare her she always joined Edith and Fräulein von Freiligrath, at their tea. To-night a bright little fire burnt in the grate, a kettle gossiped on the hob, the round table was dressed with cake and preserves; Caroline, in her blue ribbons, hovered near. "Shall we light the candles, Fräulein? Oh, here is Miss Elliott, dear Miss Elliott!" cried Edith joyfully, springing to her friend. " Do you know 'Lamentation' has kittens, and I am going to call one of them 'Joy,' and another 'Snowball?' Don't you wish Cousin Guy were here to choose the names?"

"Hush, chatterbox, and come to tea," says Anna, holding up an admonishing finger; "*Meine gute* Catherine, place the chair for Miss Elliott near the fire; she is starved with cold, and looks as though she had seen ghosts." And Anna pours out tea, and knits and prattles in a cosy fashion; and the flaxen plaits shine in the firelight.

Has she seen ghosts? What kindly spirit looks out of those glowing flames that are leaping and crackling over the logs? Humphrey's sad eyes are looking at her! No, it is years ago; she is sitting in Anna's place; she is a friendless governess, without a creature to love her but Will; some one with broad shoulders is lolling against the fireplace—a brown face, with rough tawny beard, looks round at her. "Ah, are you there my little friend?"

"I am only spinning in the moonlight," breaks in Dym quaintly. "What tale is it to be tonight, Edith?" Edith clamours for *Undine*. Fräulein tells it charmingly, and the child listens breathlessly to the pranks of Kühlchorn. "Poor Undine! it was better to be without one's soul than to suffer as she did," says Dym, with a sort of shudder, when Anna had finished.

"Not so, dear heart," returned the little German piously; "for so there would be no future for the Undine with her beloved after she had wept him to death, and the tale would lose its moral."

"But she is very unhappy in her crystal palaces," says Edith, sighing. "It is a sad story. I like the part about the dwarfs pelting each other with gold dust best."

Anna promises a more cheerful story next evening, and hums a plaintive little tune, as her needles cast off row after row. Dym knows the words that belong to it; they are Goethe's:

> Kennst Du das Land wo die Citronen blüh'n
> Im dunkeln Laub—die Gold-orangen glüh'n—

Anna misses the intermediate lines, and finishes with a sort of mellow hum—

> "Dahin—dahin,
> Möcht' ich mit dir, O mein Geliebter ziehn;"

and Dym remembers it is one of the songs Honor used to sing in the old house at Kensington.

Dym enjoys that visit to Lansdowne House. They see very little of the Delaires, who live in a fine house at Hyde Park Gate. Beatrix is mentioned as one of the great beauties of the last season. Some one says Mrs. Delaire is quite the fashion.

Dym saw Colonel Delaire riding in the Park once, and he reined up his horse when he saw the Tressilian liveries; he gave Dym a very cordial smile.

"I am glad you have got over your accident so well, Miss Elliott. Beatrix ought to have been over to Lansdowne House this week, Mrs. Tressilian, but she has been so busy, with those tableaux—she and Adelaide Beauchamp seem to have time for nothing else—though I am bound to say Miss Beauchamp is the more sensible of the two."

"What a pity her wedding is put off on account of Colonel Lintot's death, Frank!" observed Mrs. Tressilian languidly. "George seems a nice steady fellow, though he has round shoulders and stoops so dreadfully. I think Adelaide might have done better, though she is no beauty, and seems to fancy no one but George. Well, give my love to Trichy; it is a great pity she is always too busy to come and see her mother."

As Mrs. Tressilian delivers herself of this unusually long speech, she sinks back exhausted on the cushion, and Colonel Delaire canters off. As he lifts his hat, Dym sees he is getting very bald, and his face has the same pale harassed look it wore at Ingleside last Christmas. People say the beautiful Mrs. Delaire has a temper, and does not always show herself very submissive to her husband.

Dym had the good fortune to see a great deal of Will. Mrs. Chichester would send her off to spend long days with him. Dym always found him busy and cheerful, but looking thin and with a cough, and not always able to hide from her anxious eyes that his strength was not equal to his work.

That visit to London did her great good, and partly for her sake, and because her blindness made her shrink from the long winter and the emptiness of Ingleside, Mrs. Chichester made her sister promise to spend Christmas with her.

Dym was very glad to have Edith again, and to see more of Fräulein von Freiligrath. Mrs. Fortescue always cut off the ridiculous "Von;" she called it "such nonsense in a governess who has to earn her bread;" but on the whole she was far more gracious to Anna than she had been to Dym.

"*Meine Liebe*, she trains after one like a great white serpent," Anna remarked confidentially when they returned one snowy winter's night from the Vicarage, where the young people of the neighbourhood had been invited to play charades and forfeits. Humphrey had been there, and Anna had distinguished him with a great deal of artless favour; he was like Albrecht, only both Albrecht and Rudolph had great big sandy moustaches. He had a great benevolent heart, Anna was sure; and he had an empty niche in it for some one. "O thou little Marmorbild," cries Anna, embracing Dym, "this great distinguished farmer loves thee, and thou carest for him not that—nothing," snapping her little plump fingers —"forsooth, because he has rough looks and a gruff voice. Go, you are a cold-hearted girl; you do not deserve to be betrothed." Either Anna's eyes were shrewd as well as round, or Humphrey could not quite control his looks.

Dym was very glad to have Anna as companion in her walks to Woodside; it saved her a good deal of awkward embarrassment. Those walks were drawing to an end, however. Before the snow quite died off from the high land about Birstwith, gentle Esther Grey laid down the burden of her sufferings, and Dr. Grey was a widower.

Dr. Grey bore his heavy loss with fortitude, but it aged him. People said the doctor would never be the man he was again. Friends rallied round him in his trouble, and an unmarried cousin offered to keep house for him and his children: there was nothing for him but to accept it. Dym was there when she arrived. She was of French extraction, Dr. Grey told her; had lived in Rouen most of her life, and was therefore unknown to her English relations; he heard that she was a most exemplary creature, and had tended her mother lovingly to her death. Her name was Bergamotte—Louise Adrienne Bergamotte—and she had a little income of her own, sufficient to maintain herself.

"Louise was a pretty girl once, before she went over, but I do not know what she is like now. I only know she has given up her home and all her little belongings to do me and my children a kindness." And Dr. Grey, as he said this, went out sadly into the porch as he heard the sound of wheels, and Dym stationed herself and the children at the window, to watch for the first glimpse of Cousin Louise.

"Cousin Louise"—it sounded pretty. There was the fly turning the corner. Dym strained her eyes as well as she could through the darkness. There was a bird-cage at one window, with a grey parrot in it; a regular French poodle, with a tassel at the end of his tail, looked out of the other; a shrill little voice called out to the driver; a well-gloved hand handed out a bandbox, some large uncouth brown parcels, a tabby kitten, another bird-cage, and some curiously-shaped baskets.

"Is that all? Where are you, Louise?" says Dr. Grey's sad voice.

A little brown wrinkled lady, with prominent teeth and bright eyes, in a sort of yellow turban, jumps out, and kisses him on both cheeks.

"*Mon pauvre Edouard*, where are the dear children? I hope you'll not mind my bringing my parrot and Chéri. Chéri, Chéri, show yourself to this good cousin. Thou art looking thin, Edouard. Ah, the poor angel, I know all about it!" and Louise presses a little flimsy handkerchief covered with pink half crowns in good earnestness to her eyes, and then comes running in to kiss the children.

How they and Dym stare at her! So this little shrivelled bright-eyed woman is Louise. One or two of the children are afraid of her white teeth and dark face. Rupert gazes with disgust at the yellow bonnet; his dear beautiful mamma never wore such things. Louise pats them all kindly.

"You think I am Madam Wolf, my little *chou; tais-toi*, thou shalt see otherwise;" and she frisks to the great brown-paper parcels. What toys, what drums and soldiers, what gingerbread queens and wonderful confections and chocolate! The dusky little parlour quite gleams with the treasures. The children cram hands and mouth, and crowd contentedly round Cousin Louise now.

"You are the same as ever," says Dr. Grey, with a smile on his lips and something glistening in his eyes.

Louise looks up with a friendly nod. "It is all right; see, Edouard, by-and-bye these little people will love me. Now, *mon ami*, we can sit and talk."

Dym comes away presently quite contented. She and Mrs. Chichester are to go up to London the next day for the dreaded operation. When she comes again she finds Cousin Louise ruling the little household very happily. The children love her, though the boys call her "Cousin Wolf" to her face. Dr. Grey respects and confides in her. Louise wears big frills to her nightcaps when she comes out to hush some child crying in his sleep. Dr. Grey sometimes sees the little woman, in her huge brown *peignoir*, gliding with motherly face from bed to bed. She makes excellent coffee, and pours it out with a wonderful red and white fichu tied over her head. The fame of her *potage*, her *chocolat*, and excellent *confitures* reach even Mrs. Fortescue's ear. Louise concocts wonderful soup, and carries it with her own hands to the sick people, her poodle Chéri trotting after her. Louise and her grey parrot and Chéri are the delight of the village children. She is only a lean little shrivelled woman, with prominent teeth, with a shrill voice; yet Dr. Grey blesses the day when Cousin Louise came to his motherless children;

and Rupert, when he grows up, says the best friend he has, next to his father, is dear "Cousin Wolf."

If it had not been for the cause, Dym would not have been sorry to find herself back at Lansdowne House again, and in the society of the friendly Anna. It was the end of February; the worst of the winter was over. Dym carried the first snowdrop in to Mrs. Chichester on the morning they started for London.

It was with intense thankfulness that Dym wrote to Mr. Chichester a few days afterwards, announcing that the dreaded operation had turned out a very simple affair after all; both eyes had been successfully couched, and Mrs. Chichester now lay in her darkened room, exhausted and thankful, and dictating all sorts of loving messages to her son and Honor. A heap of soft pink and white wool lay on the couch beside her. Dym was always picking up stitches and rectifying rows now.

"If we work hard, do you think it will be in time?" whispered Mrs. Chichester; she was for ever holding endless confidences with her young companion on the comparative merits of fringe or tassels; all the news of the three kingdoms would not have interested the placid woman half as much as the soft ribs of the quilt that were forming under her skilful fingers; and why? Because a wonderful secret was mixed up in those skeins and balls of wool!

The little quilt lay ready and finished in the Blue Room at Ingleside long before the news came, which Mrs. Chichester was able to read for herself.

"O my dear, come here. Is he not happy? Dear, dear Honor!" And as Mrs. Chichester held out her son's letter to Dym, tears of gladness coursed down the mother's cheeks.

"Darling mother, thank God for us!" wrote Guy. "To-day they placed our little girl in my arms—such a tiny girl, with Honor's eyes. I have just kissed both mother and daughter. Honor would not rest till I laid her baby in her arms. I wish you could see my darlings together—they both look so happy. Honor sends her dear love; I will not let her excite herself by delivering a longer message."

"Is he not happy!" exclaimed the poor mother again. "Neither he nor Honor seems disappointed that it is a girl, Guy's little daughter! Well, fetch me my desk, my dear. I must write to him myself, and to Honor too."

Mrs. Chichester's cup of happiness seemed literally brimming over; the good news fully repaid her for the inevitable delay. It was the middle of April now, and Honor could not travel till the end of May. Guy wrote with some regret, a few days afterwards, that the little one was so frail that they thought it better to have her baptized by the English chaplain there. There was no time to write severally to the sponsors, but Honor wished her brother and Mrs. Chichester and Dym to stand by for the child— Humphrey was to telegraph their answer—and the doctor and his wife had promised to act as proxies. Dym was greatly moved when she heard Guy's message. To stand sponsor to his and Honor's child—to be thought worthy of such a privilege! For a little while she was almost too overcome to signify her assent. How strange that Humphrey was to stand with her! "Tell him there is nothing I would not do for you and him," she wrote in the fulness of her heart to Honor.

Guy had told them that Honor's favourite name was Florence. Florence Honor Chichester was to be the little maiden's name. Guy wrote a touching account of the whole affair. The service was held in the room adjoining Honor's, so that the mother might join in the prayers and thanksgivings. In defiance of all usages, Guy had insisted on holding his little daughter himself, and had only given her up when obliged to do so. She had cried when the clergyman touched her, but had been quite quiet and good when she was in her father's arms again, and lay cooing and opening her eyes, "just like grey flowers when the sun throws a shadow over them," wrote Mr. Chichester.

"I hope they don't let her do too much," sighed Mrs. Chichester; and Dr. Grey, when he heard of it, hoped so too.

A few days after the receipt of the last letter, Dym was sitting one evening reading to Mrs. Chichester. May had set in unusually cold and wet—a compound of March winds and April showers; this day in particular had been cold and gusty. The valley was full of driving rain, a vaporous gloom clung to the hills, the fields were steaming, a wet glistening of sunbeams had alternated for a short time at sunset, but the clouds had closed in heavily again, and the steaminess and the rain prevailed.

Mrs. Chichester shivered as Dym put down the book.

"Ring for lights, my dear, and tell Stewart to bring another log. It makes one dreary to hear nothing but the rain beating on the terrace. Just now I fancied I heard footsteps outside the window; it must have been my fancy."

"Of course it was," replied Dym cheerfully. "No one but Mr. Chichester ever goes round to the conservatory-door, and we should have heard the great door open if it had been a visitor: the idea of any visitor coming on such a night!"

"Yes, it must have been my fancy," repeated Mrs. Chichester thoughtfully. "I think the wet weather makes me nervous; everything makes me that to-day. I could almost have believed it was Humphrey coming up the terrace, the footsteps sounded so like his."

"I will ask Stewart to close the shutters, and then we shall lose that dreary patter-patter. Why, I could almost believe I heard it myself," laughed Dym; but she was nevertheless glad when Stewart appeared with the tall silver candlesticks.

"I think Phyllis wants you, miss," said Stewart, pointing over his shoulder to the hall. Was Dym getting fanciful too, or was the lad's ruddy face a little pale? "Phyllis wants you particular, miss," stammered Stewart, putting down the candlesticks awkwardly enough.

"Take care; you are dropping the wax. Why can't Phyllis come to me here, if she wants me?"

"You had better go to her, my dear," observed Mrs. Chichester, shivering and drawing her shawl close round her; "and shut the door; there seems such a draught outside."

Dym found herself in a perfect whirlwind when she left the drawing-room; and no wonder, for the conservatory-door was open, after all. Dym had half a mind to call Stewart, only she was ashamed of her fears.

"Where are you, Phyllis?" she exclaimed. "Why don't you shut that door, somebody?"

"It is only I," returned Humphrey's voice outside. "Wait in the conservatory a moment, please; I will be with you directly."

It was very mysterious, but Dym did as she was told nevertheless, and a moment afterwards Humphrey made his appearance.

"I was only speaking to Miles," he said; "you were so long in coming, my dear. Did not Stewart tell you?"

"Stewart told me Phyllis wanted me. What—what is the matter, Humphrey?" faltered Dym, growing suddenly pale over her words. Humphrey's clothes were dripping with water, the raindrops hung on his whiskers and beard, his face had a white ashen look on it, and his lip trembled strangely. "O Humphrey, I see it in your face—something dreadful has happened! Tell me quick, Humphrey, dear Humphrey," catching hold of his arm and speaking in a frightened voice. "You have heard something — Mr. Chichester — Honor — who——"

A shudder seemed to shake Humphrey from head to foot, and for a moment he held the little hands so tightly that Dym could have screamed with agony.

"Give me a moment," he gasped. "It is true. They told me so, for I could not read it for myself—Honor is dead!"

## CHAPTER III.

### THROUGH THE CROSS TO THE CROWN.

"HONOR is dead!"

When these terrible words forced themselves from Humphrey's dry lips, Dym staggered back as though he had given her a blow, and her hands fell weakly to her side.

Was this some awful delusion bred of the wild gusty evening? The conservatory-door had blown open again of its own accord; Dym's dress and hair waved in the wind; a great noise and numbness and roaring seemed in her ears; splash-splash went the rain; the drops trickled down the folds of Humphrey's dreadnought, and formed themselves into a glistening pool at his feet; the lights seemed to flicker and flash more brightly before Dym's eyes. Was she standing on firm ground? was everything tottering and reeling round her?

"It is not true," she said, putting out both hands to steady herself, and catching hold of Humphrey again.

"Don't touch me—I am wet."

How hoarse his voice sounded! He never knew why such a little thing as that should come into his thoughts. He took the girl's hands gently from his wet sleeves, and held them. Dym's white face and fixed staring eyes frightened him. A sort of hysterical cry burst from her lips.

"It is not true! O Humphrey, it can't be true! If it were it would kill him."

And she looked up pitifully into Humphrey's grey face. Her first thought was for him—not for this poor Humphrey, who stood there striving for words with which to answer her, and chafing the little hands that were not half so cold as his.

"Hush! you must not cry—not yet," he implored, as though he were speaking to a child. "We must think of him, and her too," with a look at the closed drawing-room door. "I thought I would tell you first, and then you could help me."

"Of course I will help you, if I know how," returned Dym, putting back her hair from her face in a bewildered sort of way. "I am thinking of him—I always do. I think I shall pray that he may die too! O Humphrey, you are sure it is true?"

Need she have asked? A sort of heartbroken smile wreathed poor Humphrey's lips for a moment.

"There is the telegram—read it for yourself," he said. "No, put it away; there is Madam coming," he answered hastily; and Dym glided a step or two away from him.

Mrs. Chichester looked a little taken aback when she saw the two standing together.

"Is that you, Humphrey? Why do you keep him standing there, Miss Elliott? Come in, both of you, and let him warm himself at the fire."

Humphrey cast a piteous look at his companion. He had asked her to help him.

"Come," he said; "it is no use waiting; she will see it in our faces."

Humphrey was given to meet his troubles with a dogged sort of courage, and even now it did not forsake him. Dym felt as though she were doing her part badly. He had asked her to stand by him, but as yet she had bethought herself of no way in which to assist him.

"What brings you up on such a night as this, Humphrey?" continued Mrs. Chichester cheerfully, for the prospect of a chat with her old friend was very pleasant. "I think you deserve an extra welcome for coming to see us on such an evening."

"Ay, ay, if my errand were a good one," returned Humphrey gruffly, not taking the chair to which she pointed him.

"You have bad news!" exclaimed Mrs. Chichester, suddenly changing colour as Dym had done, but speaking still in her silvery tones.

"I have," was the blunt answer.

"Then, for the love of Heaven, Humphrey, do not keep me in suspense! My boy"—catching her breath quickly—"nothing ails my boy?"

"God help your son, he has lost his wife!"

"Not our Honor?"

"Dead!" and as Humphrey uttered the monosyllable, he put his hand to his throat, as though something strangled him.

Mrs. Chichester looked at him almost vacantly for a moment, and her head moved tremulously; Dym saw the soft hands fluttering aimlessly in the air, and she knelt down and put her arms round her.

"Don't look like that; God will help him to bear it," she sobbed; "we must all pray that he may be able to bear it."

But the poor mother had not taken it in yet. "My son has lost his wife," she repeated mournfully; "my son Guy." And her hands dropped heavily into her lap; she turned with helpless scared looks from one to the other, as though beseeching them to help her.

"You have been too quick, Humphrey—she cannot understand."

But Humphrey only shook his head with a look of anguish. "I have done my best," he answered in a stifled voice. "What could I do when every word choked me? Speak to her, Miss Elliott; she is only dazed with her trouble."

But Humphrey's voice had already aroused her.

"Why do we wait? Why do we not go to him?" she suddenly exclaimed. "Dym, why do you not tell Dorothy to come to me? I must go to my son."

"Dear Mrs. Chichester—dear—dearest—you cannot go."

"Madam is right," interrupted Humphrey hoarsely; "we will be off to-night. If I travel day and night I will see my poor Duchess again. O Honor! Honor!" and Humphrey's iron face was convulsed suddenly, and he dashed away a hot drop or two with his hand as he remembered his Duchess would never come smiling to him again.

"Good Humphrey, you will take me," and the poor lady stretched out her hands to him. "I do not forget Honor is your sister, but I must go to my son. My boy is in trouble, and wants his mother—I know he will want his mother."

"She is right," Humphrey said again decidedly. "Madam is right; of course the Squire wants her, and of course she will go to him. Tell Dorothy to pack up her mistress's things. What are you looking at? you may trust her with me," he finished, with a touch of impatience, as Dym stood looking at him in helpless peplexity.

"Do what Humphrey tells you, my dear. I think God has sent him to help me." With the necessity for instant exertion, Mrs. Chichester had recovered her calmness—these mothers have such strength—her limbs still trembled strangely, and her face was deadly white; but when Dorothy came she could still give her full directions, appealing to Humphrey at every word to know if she might do this or that.

"I think I ought to take Dorothy, she may be useful;" and as Humphrey nodded, "Go up with her, my dear, and let one of the maids help; and tell Stewart to bring some coffee for Mr. Nethecote;" and as poor Humphrey shook his head with a gesture of disgust, she said reproachfully, "We must eat and drink, Humphrey, that we may have strength on the way. I want to be of use to my boy when I arrive, and you must let me take care of you too;" and the gentle creature took the rough hand and pressed it to her lips, as she repeated, "I think God has sent you to help me find my boy."

Dym left them and went upstairs, with a load of dull aching sadness at her breast. As she closed the door she heard a hoarse sob from Humphrey—one, and then another—and she knew that the unhappy brother had broken down for a minute under that touch of motherly sympathy—only for a moment, however, and then the man's intense strength forced back the anguish again. Oh, those awful tearless sobs of strong men, when some crushing sorrow is upon them—labouring sounds, rending the heart of those that hear them, but bringing no relief to the bereaved! Nature has ordained that men should be dumb in their grief: the strong crying is made in secret. Women may weep their souls away, when men only bow their heads in silence. Still are there times when the mighty avalanche of woe breaks down the barrier of reserve. I think when men weep the angels must weep with them, to see such bitter sorrow on the earth.

Poor Dym! her tears seemed dried up at

their source. They were going to him, all through the night and the driving rain, through other nights and other days, that Humphrey might see his Duchess again, and that Mrs. Chichester might comfort her son.

She had no part or lot in their trouble. Honor loved her, and Honor was lying cold in her shroud—that beautiful life was ended. The wife was snatched from her husband—the mother from her babe; the happy bride, yearning for her home, was already in the icy arms of Death. That calm beneficence, that sweet womanly presence, should bless them no longer; the brother and husband must sit broken-hearted beside their empty hearth, and who should comfort them?

Dym packed and folded, and strove to remember the little comforts that Mrs. Chichester would require on her journey. The tears were streaming down Dorothy's stern face and over Phyllis's red cheeks, but Dym had an odd lump in her throat, and a strange ringing noise in her head. " I shall never forget my little friend;" some dull echo in her brain seemed to be repeating the words over and over—" little friend—little friend." They were leaving her behind when she would have gone barefooted only to have kissed those closed grey eyes again. Hark how the wind howls, and the rain is driving across the terrace; the boughs are creaking in the garden below; doors open and bang; lights flicker and go out.

" Leave out the sealskin, Phyllis, and the rug lined with black bear," Dym says in a strange far-away voice. Where is she? Not here—not in this softly-lighted room. Her face is damp and cold, as though she is dying; dreadful shivers dart through her frame; the piercing wind is lancing her with icy knives; strange faces gibber through the darkness; the stars come out one by one. Who is this crying to her dear Lord to save her—for Death is abroad and walks the fields to-night? Something warm and loving touches her; strong womanly hands raise her up; delicious warmth tingles in her frozen veins. Who is it who wraps her in her own soft furs? who warms the stiff hands? who kisses the poor cold cheek, and lays it on her bosom? "He has sent His angel. O Honor! Honor! The one taken, and the other left."

Phyllis's rosy cheeks are quite blotched with crying; she looks at her young mistress with round frightened eyes. Dym's lips are tightly pressed together, her face looks dark and wan, and a heavy frown of pain furrows her brow.

"What are you doing, Phyllis? Mrs. Chichester will want her warm wadded cloak for to-night," she says with quick impatience. She takes the strap out of the girl's hands, and buckles it more tightly; she almost snatches the travelling cloak and bonnet and carries them downstairs.

"You have been very quick, my dear; the carriage is not round yet," says Mrs. Chichester quietly. Her soft voice and gentle movements contrast strangely with Dym's feverish eagerness. Dym notices the hands shake a little as the bonnet is adjusted; but nevertheless she makes the cup of coffee herself, and carries it round to Humphrey, and stands by him while he drinks it.

"Have you anything to say to me?" asks Dym, in her forlorn young voice. Humphrey raises his heavy eyes, and looks at her—a slim girlish figure, in a grey gown, standing under the great chandelier, with the heavy sealskin dropping out of her arms. Her eyebrows seem to frown over her great wistful eyes; a pathos of repressed impatience and trouble is in her voice.

"Come here, my dear;" and the kind hands draw her and hold her fast. "You must not fret more than you can help—remember that; but your brother will take care of you."

"Will!" Dym's face grows a little less contracted now.

"Yes, I shall send you to him. If I left you here you would make yourself sick, and that could help no one. Be brave and patient. We will write to you, Humphrey and I. You shall know all. Ah, my child, let me go. We must not say more to each other now;" and the mother's lip trembled as Dym kissed and clung to her with a sudden appreciation of that dear and tender friend.

"Take care of her, Humphrey; oh, God bless you both!" cries poor Dym. She puts up her face and kisses Humphrey, laying her innocent cheek for a minute against his, as though she can think of no other way in which to express her sympathy. The wind blows about the grey gown wildly, the lamps splutter and wave round the little shining head, a long lock of dark hair streams over one shoulder; so she stands in the halo of the lighted threshold, with the shadows creeping to her very feet; so he goes into the night and darkness, and bears her blessing with him. Hark how the storm-fiends rage above the valley; they can hear the hoarse voice of the Nid chafing against its banks; the elms are straining their mighty arms; the young rowan-trees are shivering like aspens. "There is no night there," says Dym, looking up at the angry black skies; and then she closes the door, and goes up to her room.

Mrs. Chichester had done kindly and wisely in bidding Dym go to her brother; the girl would have spent long miserable days wandering about the empty rooms and thinking of her friends. Action was a relief to her, as it is to all of us in our trouble. To sit waiting with folded hands for news that is long in coming; to watch the sorrowful faces of those we love, and see the sadness reflected in our own, and yet not to be able to minister to them or to lighten their burden,—this is the saddest part that could be allotted to us. We would fain be up and doing, going to and fro about the streets, while conventionality draws down the blinds, and hurries us into the darkened room. I wonder which of us would sit down patiently for seven days and nights with our friends, and speak out our barren human wisdom, as Job's comforters did. Nowadays the rending of garments and the sorry head-gear of ashes strike us as heathenish, though we are not yet shamed out of our sable palls and hired mourners; yet to the Jewish eyes, I suppose, the wailing and dirges of the minstrels had a fierce music of its own: it gave expression to their grief when it grew silent; it hushed the trivial platitudes of sympathy; it drowned other voices, and excited a constant tumult of regret. "To weep with them that weep." Why is it that this duty comes so hard to some of us? Why do the words falter on our lips as we take the widow's hand, or lift the fatherless child on our knee? Because words at such times are meaningless. Do we speak of comfort—can we bring the dead back again? Can we heal when He has wounded? Away with these commonplaces, these conventional speeches, that cost us so much to utter, and which do no good; rather tears, rather a strong cry of pain, than that, or a silent pressure or evidence that tells all and yet says nothing.

Dym lay and cried half the night for the loss of the friend she loved, and the sorrow that had come to those about her. She listened with a sore heart to the clock striking through the darkness as the storm lulled. When the wet grey dawn crept through the unshuttered window she woke from a miserable dream, and with aching head and trembling fingers began to dress herself hurriedly.

She had told them that she should take the early train; and when Phyllis brought her a hot cup of coffee, she found her standing by the window with her bonnet in her hand, her little trunk packed, and Kiddle-a-wink sitting on her old plaid shawl.

"You will have a wet day for your journey, miss. Miles says there's a mort of clouds to come down yet, all the more that the wind's lulled," said Phyllis, stealing a sympathizing glance to the tired face and reddened eyelids of her young mistress.

"What does it matter, Phyllis?" returned Dym listlessly; but she was glad of the coffee nevertheless. Miss Elliott was a great favourite in the household. Mrs. Bridget, the housekeeper, came up herself with the sandwiches for the young lady; even Miles, who could be high and mighty enough sometimes, thrust away his young coadjutor, Stewart, and himself put in the shawls and bags, and hoped Miss Elliott had all she wanted, and that she would not be tired by her long journey.

"Thank you, Miles, and you too, Stewart," returned Dym with her sad little smile; even the kindness of these hirelings was sweet to the poor child; even the station-master touched his hat, and said a rough word or two of sympathy.

"This is a black day in Birstwith, miss: there is not a house in the whole village that has not lost a friend. I've put the box in the van; is the dog going in with you, too?"

"Yes," returned Dym absently. Kiddle-a-wink had already established himself on the opposite seat, and was looking out of the window, lolling out his foolish red tongue. Hark, the bell was tolling the dismal news. Dym leant out for a moment eagerly, as the train moved from the platform. There was the little windy platform, with honest Dison stumping along it with a yellow dog at his heels; two children were carrying a great basket, and put it down to listen. "Mother says that's for the Good Lady," said one of them. The great rain-clouds were piling over the valley; the Nid was brawling and chafing over its boulders. There was the cottage beside the weir; it was empty still. The mill garden looked dreary. Dym shivered and threw herself back on her seat, and the long weary journey had begun.

Dym had fallen asleep, and woke up stiff and tired as the train slackened speed and drew up at the platform of King's Cross Station, with its lights and bustle and crowd of passengers and porters, which was rather a bewildering scene to Dym's sore and aching eyes. Two or three passengers looked back at the little grey-gowned lady with the grey dog under her arm; the crisp dark hair had got disarranged under the neat bonnet, and lay in stray waves over her temples; a pale wistful face looked out of the cab windows.

They were jolting into brightness again, wide shiny pavements, flaming gaslights, a jostling of foot-passengers and umbrellas across the muddy road; the omnibus horses were steaming, the shop-windows reeking with moisture, as Dym turned into Camden Town; she suddenly remembered it was Saturday night.

High Street, Camden Town, drove its usual Saturday-night traffic in spite of the wet. The cheap vendors of provisions had set up their stalls, and chaffered and cheated under the guttering tallow candles; thin women's faces hovered over the mountains of refuse fruit and inodoriferous fish; the hot-pie man drove a fierce competition with the vendor of kidney potatoes; two or three coalheavers—temperance men—were scalding themselves with cups of hot coffee; some ragged boys had collected round an apple-stall; the butchers' shops were flaring to the tune of "Come, buy, buy;" a few slouching figures came out from the swing-doors of the great shining gin-palaces.

Dym looked out with amazed eyes; this was one of the phases of life in the great Saturday-night babel. A hungry face or two, thin shawls and draggled gowns, a hubbub of voices, of straggling hoofs, then the dark bridge and the canal, more stalls and shops and brightness, a quiet corner with some almshouses, and a clock striking, the rain splashing down on the empty pavement and on the iron railway, and down into the areas of modest villas, and on the snowy steps of No. 3, Paradise Row.

Dym paid the man and ran in, with a hasty nod to Mrs. Maynard. It was Saturday night, and she knew she should find Will at home.

The cheerful glow of a little fire shone through the half-opened door; but the candlesticks were on the table, still unlighted. Will was not poring over his books or papers as usual. The tea-things were at one end, still untouched; a kettle sung cosily on the hob; there was a curious faint smell of ether in the room, and Will was in his easy-chair half asleep before the fire.

He did not rise when Dym came in, but only held out his hand to her with a look of extreme surprise.

" My dear child, why did you not let me know you were coming up; who would have thought of seeing you to-night?" but his look seemed to say she was very welcome.

" Were you asleep, Will?"

" I believe I was"—yawning and stretching himself—" I thought it was part of my dream when you came in and woke me. What time is it, Dym, and when did you arrive in London?"

" I have only just come on from King's Cross. What is the matter, Will?—you look pale." Dym was keeping her own face out of sight, while Mrs. Maynard lighted the candles and bustled about the room.

" Mr. Elliott has not been well. I think he has wanted you, miss. You have been sleeping finely, sir, for I opened the door once or twice very quietly, and you never heard me, nor Dick neither; but Dick creeps about like a little mouse."

" Not well, Will?"

" A return of my old pain; never mind, I am better now. Make my sister some tea, Mrs. Maynard. And take off your bonnet, Dym, and sit down by the fire; I can't see you while you are standing behind me." And he took down a very cold little hand from his shoulder, and put her in front of him.

" O Will, how dreadfully white you look, and your lips are quite dark! I could not half see you before."

" Pooh! nonsense; the pain is gone; I am only stupid from my long nap."

But Dym noticed that he spoke feebly, and raised himself with difficulty.

" You are not much to look at yourself, Dym; why, foolish girl, there are positively tears in your eyes. Indeed, I am better now."

" Yes, I know, Will, but it is not that; we have had such terrible news from Mentone; and Mrs. Chichester and Humphrey went last night; and they left me alone, and—and——" but Dym could not speak any more for crying.

" You need not tell me; I know, I can guess," returned Will quickly. Dym had put down her head on his knee, and she did not see the strange look that came over his face; one hand was hidden for a long time within his waistcoat, and his lips drew darker, and his breath was drawn with difficulty for a moment. " I knew it must come," he muttered when the paroxysm had passed, and he wiped the cold perspiration that stood in drops on his forehead. Will was used to these attacks now; but he was, nevertheless, very glad that Dym's face was hidden on his knee.

" Oh, Will, how could you know? It seems all so sudden and dreadful; just when he—when they were so happy."

Will pressed his hand heavily on Dym's head.

" Yes, it is just that. How mysterious are His ways! Poor Chichester! it will go hardly with him, I fear. Only one year of happiness, and a lifetime of regret. How strange that you should have come and told me this to-night!"

"Why to-night, dear?"

"Because—because—well, I will not tell you; I have queer thoughts sometimes. I did not want you to say it out; I seemed to know all about it, as though I had expected it all my life long."

"Dear Will, it is not like you to be fanciful; how could you know that Honor was dead?" and Dym's lips parted anxiously as she looked at him. Will was hardly like himself to-night.

He answered her with a smile, half sweet, half sad—

"Dym, do you believe in dreams?"

"Why, no, Will, of course not."

"I used to say the same," he continued musingly. "Daniel was a man of dreams; but then he was 'greatly beloved.' I wonder, if we kept our hands and hearts pure, whether our guardian angel might sometimes come and whisper them to us. I had a strange dream once."

"You have never told it to me, Will."

"I never spoke of it to any one. I was afraid to breathe it even to myself. I seemed asleep and yet awake. It has haunted me ever since."

"You will tell it to me, dear?"

"When I woke it seemed to me as though the meaning was quite clear. Such a beautiful life could not die out without a sign. He thought he had her safe, poor wretch; one might as well have tried to detain an angel." He seemed as though he were speaking to himself, but Dym held her breath, quite awe-struck, as she listened.

"This angel must have had a woman's face, for the hand was hers. Perhaps you are right, and I am fanciful; but your news has not surprised me."

"You forget; I have told you nothing, Will."

"Nothing but what I knew. How did it happen? Is the child alive? I hope so, for Chichester's sake."

"Indeed we don't know," returned Dym, weeping; "the telegram said nothing but that she was gone. Humphrey said he must set out at once, and so did Mrs. Chichester; they have both promised to write and tell us all."

"And you have heard nothing?" returned Will, disappointed; "you don't know even whether she took her child with her or left it to comfort him. She would rather do that, I know. I wish Mentone were not so far off, and that I could go to him."

"Oh, Will, if you only could go!"

"What would be the good of it to either of us? He would wring my hand and look me in the face, but he would say no word to me. I should not dare to speak to him, he would be so hard and fierce and speechless in his misery."

"You are the only one to whom he would listen."

Will shook his head. "I tell you no, Dym; if he opened his mouth to me it would be to rail against Heaven, and curse his fate. Poor Chichester! we must pray for him; but no spoken sympathy can avail him."

"And his mother?"

"He is beyond her now; he will put away her arms from about him and say terrible words, and go away and shut himself up with his dead. Her tears will craze him. She will want him to eat and drink, and to keep his miserable life in him; and one of these days, when it grows too intolerable, he will leave you all."

"Oh, Will, cease, cease; you frighten me."

"He will come back, my girl," returned Will, looking at her with his gentle smile. "I know him so well. These noble souls are not left to wander away into outer darkness. Do you remember the story of Sintram, Dym, and how the Lady Verena prayed for him from behind her convent grating? Don't you think that a wife in Paradise prays for her husband on the earth?"

"Do you think so, Will?"

"My child, why should we doubt? There are sudden horizons, where heaven and earth seem to touch and mingle. We believe 'in the communion of saints.'"

"Do you really think she will watch over him, Will?"

"You would call me fanciful again if I were to tell you some of my thoughts. We are getting too material nowadays, Dym, and so the finer voices get hushed out of the universe. We talk too much, and listen too little."

Dym sat on the ground, with her earnest face propped on her hands; her bonnet had fallen off, and her hair fell into dark shining waves. What a childish sweet face it was, in spite of its paleness and tear-stains! Something pathetic in Dym's attitude seemed to strike Will, and he suddenly bent down and kissed her forehead.

"My poor tired little Dym!"

"It rests me so to hear you talk, Will."

He gave her a full bright smile of understanding.

"I think we have talked enough now. Pour out the tea, Dym, and give me a cup; I must go out directly."

"To-night?" exclaimed his sister in surprise; "there is no service."

"The boys will be practising, though. No, don't keep me," as though he anticipated the remonstrance on Dym's lips; I must go down to the church to-night." And Dym knew him too well to venture on raising an objection.

She waited for him to come back until she was tired.

Kiddle-a-wink had curled himself on his chair and had gone to sleep, and Dym had fallen into a half doze over her sad thoughts; she was thinking what Will had said about Guy Chichester, and longing, with a vain fruitless longing, to see him again, and judge for herself how he looked. "Do the finer voices get hushed?" she thought, with a dreamy remembrance of Will's speech. "If I held my breath and listened, could I hear Honor's voice?" and it almost seemed to the weary girl as though Honor's beautiful face were growing out of the stillness and firelight: the frank sweet eyes, the powerful gentle brow, the lips closely folded, yet smiling. "I will do anything for you and him," Dym seemed to be saying; and Honor, or somebody else, answered, "By-and-bye."

"How long you have been, Will!" opening her eyes wide as Will came in and closed the door softly after him.

He came up to her side with a face of grave brightness.

"What, up still, naughty child? I thought you would have gone to bed long ago; do you know it is eleven o'clock?"

"I am very tired," returned Dym sleepily; "where have you been all this time, Will?"

"Where should I have been?" he returned quietly; "the church was nice and warm, so you need not be afraid of my vigil; the rain has stopped too; and there is such a moon!" and Will's face seemed almost to reflect some of its light still; it dazzled Dym, holding her chamber candlestick, and looking at him through half-closed eyes.

"Try and sleep well, precious child; we must both try to gain strength for to-morrow. I have been making up my mind to-night that I must tell you something that you ought to know; but to-morrow will do. My poor Dym," holding her very tightly for a moment, "you are very fond of your old Will Conqueror, as you call him."

Dym's eyes were not a bit drowsy now.

"Well, I would not have you love me less, if it caused you ever so much sorrow. God means us to love each other, and so to draw each other up: we must still keep hold of the 'silver cord,' though it is loosed sometimes."

"I wish I were as good as you, Will," returned the girl humbly. She did not understand him in the least, only in a vague sort of way she thought how Will's sweet nature seemed to distil even the bitterness out of sorrow itself; he had taken her news with the air of a man who is given to look out gravely at life. The terrible surprise had hardly elicited an exclamation; throughout their talk he had sat dreamy—self-absorbed—with the wondering look of one who is dealing with mysteries.

Dym was too weary even for sorrow to-night; she crept up to her little garret, next to Dick's, who chirped out a good-night to her as she passed, and had soon forgotten her own and other people's troubles.

As Will closed the door after her a little of the brightness died out of his face, and he sat down sighing in his easy-chair.

He had been praying for Guy Chichester to-night, wrestling for him as he had never wrestled for himself; the links that had bound these two men together had never been stronger than to-night. Will felt a strange intense longing to press his friend's hand again, and look into his dark grief-worn face; while Guy, stretching out his arms over his dead wife's face in the fierce writhings of despair, thought that there was only one voice he could bear to hear in his misery, and that was Will's.

Will raked up the dying embers of the fire again and fed it with fresh fuel; he had much to do to-night. With the clearness and perspicuity that sometimes come to us under the influence of some great emotion, he had set himself to review his past life: again the years passed before him, one after the other, each with its several marks of joy and sorrow, with its burden of sins and regrets. Had it been such a sad life after all? There were aspirations unfulfilled, hopes disappointed, patience struggling with regret; the breaking out of a sudden pain and longing that had drowned his soul in terror; trouble had come to him, and toil and suffering; but the dominant calm of his nature had endured all and prevailed.

He had not always been unhappy, even when his trouble threatened to overwhelm him. The storm had beaten over and around him, but within there was peace, the peace of a quiet conscience, of a steadfast performance of daily duty done with such measure of strength that had come to him.

He remembered how in his boyhood he had longed to do something heroic, something out of the common ways of men, that should place his feet among the heroes. Dym's name of Will Conqueror had pleased this fancy, and he smiled sadly to himself to think how the youthful ambition had died away.

And yet, in his humble way, had he not strove to the utmost? He had not fought with dragons, perhaps, but he had battled with hydra-headed monsters of disease and ignorance. He had proved his virgin armour in foul dens, and the noxious breath of the fierce reptiles had overborne his young strength; had he not come out wounded, and bearing honourable scars from the conflict? was he not bearing them now?

"I have done so little; it has been so short, after all; I have not earned my rest," he thought sadly, and his head drooped on his breast. Will it be so with all of us when we cast up our poor blotted accounts, and see the sorry sum-total of our good deeds? So much for good intentions—whole pages, hundreds, perhaps; such a thin sprinkling of actions really performed, of good thoughts really lived.

Here was a pure nature crying woe to itself, because the weakness of its will had sometimes betrayed it; because he had called out at times upon his loneliness, and wished that his hearth-fires had burnt more brightly.

He remembered how an old pauper had recognised this instinct of longing once.

"We have all our troubles to bear," he had said to her, as he sat beside her in the great whitewashed ward, listening to her dismal category of woes—Jem was at sea, and Susan was too poor to come to her; and it was hard dying with naught but strange faces about her. "One may have food and raiment, and yet feel sad and lonely at times." Something in the patient tones seemed to touch her; she was a hard, battered-looking woman, with a tanned face and bristling grey hair, and Will's face looked strangely youthful beside hers.

"Ay, ay, we all have our troubles, paupers as well as gentlefolks; thou'rt a lad to be a parson; thou'rt the sort women love; but I'm thinking the Lord loves thee too, and He wont let thee be long lonesome."

Was not old Susan right? had it been long, after all? would he change his lot with Guy Chichester? No, a hundred times no.

"'He doeth all things well.' Why have I been so impatient, so distrustful? He has made this pain easy to bear—a joy almost. 'Lord, now lettest thou thy servant'"—we can guess how the humble soul chanted his *Nunc Dimittis*. Unhappy!—the length and breadth and depth of his peace seemed to flood the poor room with light; he stretched himself on his bed with a smile on his face; he was tired, and the morrow's work was before him. "I think I shall sleep now," thought Will, as he turned his face to the wall; and almost before the words left his lips he slept.

That night William Elliott had another dream. He thought he was standing on a strange place, neither land nor water, but on some shifting substance that gave way beneath his feet. A heavy burden was on his back, something that trailed behind him and dragged him back, and yet he dared not try to free himself.

"I am so tired of it all," he heard himself say; and the sound of his voice seemed to echo strangely; "so tired of it all."

"Conqueror, and tired!" said a voice that thrilled him strangely. "Look here!" and suddenly the weight slipped from him. At his feet lay a broken cross, and a crown of scarlet rowan-berries lay beside it; but as he stooped and picked it up, they changed and brightened into gold.

## CHAPTER IV.

### "QUI PATITUR VINCIT."

HERE are days which, in spite of all their sadness, we would give worlds to live once more.

Dym would have given a good year out of her life if she could have had that Sunday over again.

Life has such terrible surprises; now and then its mysteries are so cruel. If we could only lift the veil just a little; see the sand that is ebbing from the hour-glass: watch the clear steady strokes of the scythe, that is coming our way perhaps; "if we had only known, we should have done so differently," we say.

Ah, that is just it! We come down one morning a little listless, a trifle out of humour; the day goes on; we laugh and talk, we are moody or discontented; we waste our time in trifles, in looking up vacantly at passing clouds, and we do not know that the hours of one we love are numbered; that to-day, or to-morrow, or the next day, we shall say a good-bye that will wring our hearts with the remembrance. If we had known—if we had only known!

This Sunday rose with a misty brightness on

it, a soft vaporous light, neither gloom nor sunshine; the pavements were washed clean, little gleams and hints of water glittered under hollow stones and down garden-paths; the spring flowers were prematurely faded. William Elliott and his sister looked regretfully at the clumps of battered tulips and narcissus in the little three-cornered garden belonging to the sexton. St. Luke's bell was clanging out with a sturdy wiry sound; in the distance other bells chimed in, in various tones; a few young people were already gossiping in front of the Independent chapel; the minister, a great burly man with a red beard, came round a corner, swinging his arms like pump-handles, and nodded to Will. Will seemed to have a word of greeting for every one he passed —for a friendly omnibus-driver, for a couple of porters off duty, for the old man at the crossing; by-and-bye he stopped to speak to a few loiterers in the Malden Road.

"If I were you, lads, I would not trouble those bells to ring for nothing," he said, halting, and looking at them with shrewd kindly eyes. One of the youths, who was better dressed than his companions, blushed and looked at Dym.

"Mother goes to chapel," said another sturdily.

"Church or chapel; but it is the dear old Mother Church that is calling to us all so loudly just now. Come, lads, six days for yourselves, and one for the God who made you." And to Dym's surprise three out of the four sheepishly followed them, and the young schismatic remained discontentedly, kicking his heels against the wall.

Will left Dym to show the boys to their places, after which she went to her favourite seat under the west window; the old blind man had long ago been gathered to his fathers, but a white-headed sweeper occupied his place. A watery sunbeam or two was shivering against the pillars, and kindling the violet and blue robes in the Evangelist window—the altar was in shadow—all dull reds and faint golds. Will looked shadowy and white as he came out of the vestry; the organ played on in sweet minor chords. Dym, standing up with set lips and wistful far-away eyes, suddenly remembered how a brown hand, with an odd-shaped Oriental ring on it, had in that very place been laid on her book, and how she had flushed up with surprise and pleasure, and left off singing.

Dym could not sing now, not a note, there was such a tangle of pain and weariness in her heart; the words came to her ears with a jangle of meanings and repetitions. " We have erred and strayed," prayed Will. Dym knelt in her place, dumb and motionless. " Comfort him, only comfort him, and let little Florence live;" she blended this petition somehow with every response in the Litany, she sang it silently in every line of the hymn; " comfort him, comfort them all." Was there any other prayer worth praying?

" For all that are desolate and in trouble—perhaps, when she comes to that, she may think of me," sighed poor Humphrey.

Will read the prayers and preached. Mr. Benedict was away. There was to be a charity sermon in the evening, somebody said, and the chaplain of the almshouses was to deliver it.

Dym listened in a stupid sort of attention at first; she thought it odd that Will should be preaching a funeral sermon, till she remembered he had told her of rather a sudden death that had occurred in the parish.

A woman, comparatively young, had died, leaving six children motherless behind her; the widower was sitting in a pew to the right of Dym, with the two eldest children beside him; the bigger girl was looking at the crape tucks in her frock, and the younger had hold of her father's hand. As Dym watched the little group she strove to clear her mind and listen.

Afterwards, when she would have given worlds to recal that sermon, she could only bring up disjointed sentences—a word here and there. She had a vague sense of standing out on a mountain-top, she was on tiptoe, giddy and breathless; suddenly a door opened, somewhere up above in the blue infinite. Were those the white-robed multitudes Will was talking about? Was Honor amongst them? were those the wives in Paradise who were praying for their husbands?

"Don't cry, papa," she heard a little voice say near her. A man's head went lower and lower, a dark cropped head, not a brown curly one; broad shoulders, that somehow remind her of Guy, heaved and shook in repressed agitation. "Now unto Him who is able to keep us from falling," comes in a strange falter from Will's lips, the organ breaks into sad minor chords again, and the people stream out. Dym's veil falls over her face as she stands in the empty church, listening to the dirge-like music and watching a streak of lilac sunshine in the chancel; the widower has gone out, with his little girl's hand still clinging to his. Her crape tucks are crumpled already, though her sister's are quite fresh. She has a tender old-fashioned face that lingers in Dym's memory.

"Are you ready, my dear?" says Will, limping up to her with a tired face. "I have two or three people to see on our way home."

Dym, who is restless, prefers waiting for him instead of sitting alone in the little parlour. She watches him diving down area-steps or stumbling up wooden staircases with undiminished activity.

"Sunday is your hardest day; but I have never seen you look more weary," she says to him, when at last he has finished and turned his steps to Paradise Row.

Yes, he is tired, too much so to eat, in spite of his efforts. He is getting a battered old Conqueror now, he tells her. He says it with a sudden sweet smile that brings the odd feeling into her throat again. Dym sits dull and listless when he goes out to the schools presently; the sunbeams have gone in, the afternoon is full of grey neutral tints. Dym's pale face and grey gown, and Kiddle-a-wink's rough coat, seem all in unison. Some pallid sunset clouds are setting westward. "This is more like November than

May," Dym thinks; and then she remembers with an inward shiver that this is Guy Chichester's wedding-day.

What is he doing? What are Mrs. Chichester and Humphrey doing? How far had they got on that weary journey of theirs? Dym's mind is travelling on with them while she sits by the little window in Paradise Row gazing vacantly out on the passers-by. The children troop in by twos and threes from the Sunday-school. Little Dick Maynard clatters by on the pavement, and pulls off his old cap when he sees Dym. The children gather in bands and look shyly down the street; a slight bowed figure comes in sight, with a dying flare of red clouds behind him. There is a little commotion, a dropping of curtseys. Will comes up among them limping in his hasty way. Tired as he is, he has a word and smile for them. "Now, Dimples, a cup of tea, for I must be back in the vestry by half-past six; one of the choir-boys has got into mischief." And Will sinks into his easy-chair with a long sigh of relief.

"I have not had a word with you to-day, Will," said Dym reproachfully, as they hurried through the streets again.

Will suddenly turned and held out his hand to her.

"It is all in the day's work, my dear. But I have saved an hour out of it for you."

"But not to-night, Will. I am not so selfish as to ask you to talk to me to-night."

"I wish it, dear; it is the hardest bit of duty

that is left for me yet. I want you to be brave and help me to do it."

"Help you, Will?"

"Yes, my child." But he said no more, and Dym went and sat for a long half-hour in the dimly-lighted church, wondering why Will had asked her to help him, and what he would have to tell her that would be so hard in the telling.

And the real truth never entered into Dym's head for a moment. Will read the prayers again, but a stranger preached; afterwards they had that wonderful hymn, "The Pilgrims of the Night," which she remembered was Guy Chichester's favourite:

> Faith's journey ends in welcome to the weary,
> And heaven, the heart's true home, will come at last.

Dym's mind was full of one poor weary pilgrim, when, looking up, she saw Will was not standing in his place, but kneeling low, with hidden face, and his hands stretched out on the desk before him.

Dym waited for him as usual in the porch; she was quickening her steps, for the evening was chilly, but he detained her. "Not so fast; there is no hurry, now. Look up there," and Will pointed to the dark sky above their heads, gemmed over with quivering points and sparkles of light. "I am so glad we can see the stars to-night."

"Why, Will?" Dym was for hurrying on again, but he drew her arm through his.

"I have an odd fancy for starlight on Sunday

evening—those many twinkling eyes always recal to me 'the great cloud of witnesses.' I am glad, too, we had that hymn to-night. I wish Chichester could have heard it."

Dym's reply was scarcely audible.

"I thought of another little pilgrim while they were singing it, and wondered where her 'weary steps' would turn by-and-bye. I have been thinking of you on and off all day."

"Of me?" There was certainly a little reproach in Dym's tones; she thought there were others of whom he might have been thinking to-day.

"I have not forgotten them either"—as though he understood the implied rebuke—" somehow my heart feels large enough to take in the whole world; you will know presently why I think of you most to-day."

There were in one of the by-streets leading out of the Malden Road, when all at once Will stopped, and she felt his arm press heavily against hers.

"What is the matter, Will?" for though it was too dark to distinguish his face, she could hear a quick pant, almost a groan. "Is it the pain again?"

"Yes; I must walk slower. Don't speak to me—not this minute, Dym. I shall be better directly." But Dym noticed that he leant on her more heavily every minute, and that he could hardly drag himself up the few steps that led to their door.

"Dear Will," this cannot be your old pain,"

she said anxiously, as she watched him sink wearily into his chair.

Will shook his head, and motioned her to give him a little bottle that stood near. A blue livid look had come over his face, and the lips had the same dark colour that had startled Dym yesterday. The breath seemed to come in heavy pants for a moment, and then the oppression left him, and he opened his eyes and looked at Dym, who was kneeling beside him, trying to chafe his cold hands.

"My poor little Dym, I did not mean you to see this. Give me a few more drops, dear; I shall be able to talk presently."

"You must not, Will; it will make you worse;" and tears gathered slowly to Dym's eyes—she had never seen him look so bad as that.

"By-and-bye," he repeated, and then he seemed to doze.

Dym noiselessly fed the fire, and sat herself down to watch him. Tired! He was wearing himself out; the colourless face looked quite sharply cut and haggard against the dark cushion; the mouth had its usual sweet look, but the brow was contracted and furrowed with pain. Dym wondered why she had never noticed that Will was growing grey. His fair hair had quite a silvery gleam in it in the lamplight.

One thin hand lay over the side of his chair. Dym's lips twitched once or twice as she sat looking at him, with a dull ache and vague uneasiness in her heart. Was he ill? Was that what he was going to tell her? Anything but that! "O Will, Will, I could not bear you to be ill now, when I want you so;" and Dym's head drooped with the very thought.

It was quite late, almost midnight, when he woke and declared himself refreshed.

"And you have been watching me all this time! How kind of you, Dym, and how tired you must be!"

But Dym did not feel sleepy to-night, so she told him: "I am quite wakeful, too much so for my own comfort. Do you really think you are better, dear?"

"The pain has left me," he returned evasively, as Dym put back the damp hair from his forehead. "Dym, do you think it would be too late to give me some tea? I always wake so thirsty after one of these attacks."

"Too late? of course not;" and Dym bustled off with some feint of cheerfulness. The little kettle seemed always singing in the curate's room; it quite bubbled over in its cosy content now. Dym made the tea and brought it to Will.

"This seems like old times," he said, looking gratefully in her face. "Are you sure you are not tired? You must have some tea too. Do, to please me, Dym;" and Dym made a great effort and swallowed some.

"Now put your head down here," drawing her with weak hand among his cushions. "You wont hurt me, and I can talk better so. Tell me, darling, have you any idea why I'm thinking of you so to-night?"

"Don't, Will." Somehow his words seemed to hurt her with a sudden sharp pain; she put out her hand to stop him, but Will carried it to his lips.

"I would save my child from this if I could. God knows I would willingly have gone on a little longer for your sake, Dym—only for your sake; but I feel it is not to be, dear; you must make up your mind to part with your poor old Conqueror."

"Never, never! What are you talking about? Hush, I will not listen! O Will, Will!" and Dym stretched out her arms to him with a piteous entreaty for him to stop.

"Dearest, I must say it—it would be cruel kindness to withhold it now. I know I cannot live very long, Dym."

"Who says so?—they dare not say so. I will not believe it—I will not, I will not;" and Dym's wild words came through her clenched teeth in strange vehement tones. Believe that Will, her Will, could ever leave her? The girl's shrill young voice filled Will's tender heart with dismay and anguish.

"Do you want me to stay in this weary world, my dear?" he said almost reproachfully. "I think I am getting too weak and tired for my work. What was it they were singing to night, Dym, darling? 'Faith's journey ends in welcomes to the weary!' Would you deprive me of such a welcome as that?"

"Hush, hush! I want you, Will. O Will, I love you so—I love you!" and the unhappy girl threw her arms round his neck and held him almost frantically.

"This is the hardest work of all," murmured poor Will. "O my child, be brave, and help me to bear it!"

"I cannot," came sullenly from Dym's lips. She was almost beside herself.

"Not if it makes me worse to see you like this? I have so little strength, and this wastes it terribly;" and again the ominous darkness came to his lips, and the poor over-worked heart laboured and strained bravely to do its part.

"Some more drops," he said faintly; "don't be frightened, I am better again; only we must talk more quietly; lay your head down again, I like to feel it there. When you were a child you always came to your poor old Conqueror to be petted."

"Will, you are breaking my heart!" She could not have helped that cry if her life or his had depended on it. Perhaps he hoped to move her to tears by the tenderness of his words; perhaps he guessed at the spasm that contracted her throat, and knew the pent-up feelings must have some outlet. Already her breast was heaving with repressed sobs; she clung to him more quietly now, and the tears rained over his hands.

"That is right: cry, it will do you good, and by-and-bye you will be able to listen to me—we must have some long talks together. Dym, darling, you know I love you too."

"But not so much as I do you. O Will, not half so much, not half so much!"

"Do I not, dear? Nay, you are mistaken; you have been dearer to me than any one thing —except—but we will not talk of that. If it had been His will I would almost have been glad to live a little longer for your sake. You believe this, dear?"

She nodded as though words were impossible.

"When I knew that I had heart disease, my first thought was to keep it from you. I knew you would never be happy for a moment away from me. I thought I would spare you months, perhaps years of needless anxiety."

She left off sobbing to listen. Perhaps he was not going to die yet—not just yet.

"This is why I did not give you my reason for refusing to leave St. Luke's. There were other difficulties, but for your sake I might have conquered them; only I knew, I knew it would be useless pain to give up my work. You understand me, dear—you do not think I am wrong now?"

"Wouldn't it have made you better?" she whispered.

"No, my child," he replied firmly; "dismiss that idea from your mind for ever. The disease under which I am labouring admits of no human remedy: it is a worn-out heart, Dym, and nothing will make it work properly, though Dr. Lever says I may live perhaps for years."

"Then why—why did you not come up there and rest?"

"Because I did not believe him. No, my child, there are no years in prospect for me. I have suffered too much, gone through too much.

I shall not have to bear much more. O Dym, try to be glad for me; I am longing so sorely for my rest."

She only shook her head and buried her face deeper in the curtains. Glad! how could she be glad, even for his sake? The welcomes might be sweet to the faithful servant, but death itself seemed so terrible to this poor child, stretching out her tender arms to detain the brother who was so dear to her.

"Will, do not leave me; pray that you may not leave me!" clinging to him with one cold little hand, and speaking in such a weary voice.

"Would it help either of us? Dear, I must go or stay, just at His bidding. I am ready to suffer a little more, or I am ready to go to-night."

"I always knew you were too good for this world, Will," exclaimed the weeping girl. But Will silenced her gently.

"Hush! you must not say that: you would not pain me if you could help it, would you? He is more merciful to us than we are to ourselves. He will not remember our failures. I have done so little, and He has done so much."

There was a moment's silence, and then he put his hand fondly on her head.

"Why do you keep your face hidden, Dimples? I want to see it again." Ah, the old pet name, the dear old childish name!

"I am so sorry you cannot love Humphrey, my pet; he would have taken such care of you."

"Please don't speak of that to-night, Will."

"Very well" (holding the sad little face

between his hands for a moment and looking at it with wistful tenderness); "I should like to feel somebody was taking good care of my child for ever and always. But it can't be helped. I know Mrs. Chichester will always be your friend."

"Don't mind about me; nothing will matter then." Dym was feeling for words to-night, but her pain choked them back. He might talk to her, but in her anguish how was she to answer him? Even Guy Chichester faded from her thoughts in the prospect of this new trouble.

"It has all been so sudden. To-morrow, if God wills, we will talk of this again. Now go to bed, my darling; it is nearly three o'clock."

"No, no," she implored; "I would rather stop with you to-night. I could not sleep. Let me sit and watch you, Will, as I did before. Only to-night—only just to-night."

"My precious child, it goes hard with me to refuse you; but indeed it is better not. I think I could sleep now myself, and your presence will only keep me restless."

"Shall you go to bed, Will?"

"I think I must; my limbs ache so, and I feel strangely weary. This has taken it out of me. You will be good and brave, and try to sleep, Dym."

A faint misty smile answered him. "God bless my child!" was all he said; but he held her tightly for a moment, as though he were not willing to let her go, and in the silence his lips moved as though he were invoking a blessing. But when she reached the door he called her back to him and blessed her again and again, and told her hurriedly that she must be comforted, for he would love her dearly—dearly, wherever he was. And so he sent her away.

But when she had closed the door he sank down heavily in his chair, and bowed his head upon his breast. He was tired—strangely tired, he repeated. This had been the hardest work that he had had to do, and it had gone hardly with them both.

As he sat there in the darkness—for the lamp was flickering low—the words "O Will, I love you so—I love you so!" seemed ringing in his ears; again he felt her girlish arms round his neck and her tears wetting his breast, and the damp soft hair resting against his cheek. "O merciful All-powerful, comfort my child!" he groaned. And some voice out of the weird silence seemed to answer, as it had done before, "Not now, but presently;" and as this made itself heard within his heart, the tranquil soul found peace.

"I must lie down and get an hour's rest," he thought; but some strange torpor oppressed him, and he felt unable to move. "'Watch for me by the golden gate.' I wonder if she will be there?" was his last conscious thought before he slept. The dying brands of the fire flared up for a moment and smouldered to decay; the lamp spluttered and hissed, and finally went out; Kiddle-a-wink stretched himself on the rug with a low whine, as though some dream had disturbed him; but still Will slept on.

Upstairs Dym was tossing and weeping on

her pillow, and praying impotent prayers; outside the cocks were crowing, a faint windy dawn stirred in the quiet streets, the stars were paling and dying out, and the quiet figure still sat on in the darkened room below.

"Let us go that we may awaken him out of sleep," said the loving friends of old. Alas, none but One could awaken William Elliott now!

Dym, waking out of the troubled sleep that had come to her from very weariness of sorrow, heard some strange stir and movement, that seemed to reach her in her dreams. Somewhere, far off, Dick was crying. A voice said "Hush!" A man's footstep went hurriedly to and fro. Dym threw something round her, and ran down; some terrible fear was clutching at her heart; she would have called out "Will!" but her voice failed her.

The little household, huddled together, saw her advancing on them, slim and white, and looking before her with the fixed dilated eyes of a sleep-walker; and honest Richard Maynard put out his hand, with something like a sob, to stop her. "No, don't go in there; my missis here wants to talk to you."

"I know," replied Dym, in an odd far-off voice. She put aside the brawny arm with a little cold hand and pushed through them. Dick fell over one of his crutches, and began to cry again; and Susan threw her apron over her head. "Ah, lackaday! the poor young lady, what will we do with her, Richard?" And Richard drew his rough sleeve before his eyes.

Know—did she know what awaited her? The blind had been pulled up; a May sun shone merrily into the window; Kiddle-a-wink was whining and smelling restlessly about the bowed figure that sat in the easy-chair, with its thin hands clasped before it, and a smile on the white face that rested so peacefully among the cushions. There, where he had parted from her last night, there he sat, dead; but still she made no cry or sign that she understood. She bent over and kissed him with a face that was almost as grey and corpse-like as his, then closed the glazed eyes, and laid the heavy head upon her bosom. Dead! of course he was dead; and she was dying too. It was Richard Maynard who saw the awful shadow in her face and caught her as she fell; it was he who freed the hands from their fond clutch, and laid the smiling face back on its pillow, and carried the girl up to her little room, and left her with Susan crying plentiful tears over her.

Dym's head was lying on the faithful creature's lap, when she woke from her swoon. Dym held out her arms to Richard Maynard to carry her down again when he came in next to inquire after her. "I dare not. You must help her, Susan; she bean't fit for anything but bed now."

"I must go to Will, and you must take me," answered Dym in her feeble voice. "Good Richard, dear Richard, carry me down. Susan, ask him to do it. I cannot leave Will alone."

Richard fairly turned his face to the wall and sobbed, as the girl set forth her miserable little petition. She was hysterical after that, and Susan had her way, and tucked her up in her little bed, and drew down the blinds and sat beside her. Heaven only knows the anguish with which Dym lived through those first few hours. She lay staring at the wall with blank dark eyes, when Susan hoped she was sleeping. Now and then she would throw out her arms and bury her face in the pillow, as some intolerable remembrance came to her mind; then she would feel Susan's rough hand smoothing her hair. She wanted to be alone—she wanted it with a fierce longing that nearly drove her frantic—but she lacked energy to say so. When the doctor—a white-headed old man—came to her bedside and took her hand (he was an old friend of Will's), she drew it away almost angrily.

"What do you want? Who sent for you? who gave you leave to disturb me?" she said in a quick vehement way.

The old man understood the girl's despair too well to take umbrage at it; he answered her with fatherly kindness—

"You are not well, my dear. These good people sent for me. You must be patient, and try and bear your trouble—we all must, you know."

"Can you do any more for Will? have you been to him?" pushing back her hair and looking at him with strained, bloodshot eyes.

He shook his head.

"No one can do any more for him, my child; he is beyond our help now."

"Then you can do nothing for me. I am well, quite well; only I shall want him all my life long," she said, bursting into tears and falling back on her pillow.

It was evening before they left her alone. Susan thought she had fallen asleep at last, and had gone down to sit with her husband a little; but Dym, who had been lying perfectly motionless watching the creeping shadows on the ceiling, suddenly sat up, and then began groping her way down the dark staircase. She had told them in a fierce sort of way that she was well; but as she dragged herself along she felt as though she had risen from a long illness; her limbs ached strangely; her head felt curiously light and confused; every now and then a faintness seemed creeping over her, and she clung to the crazy baluster with both hands.

The house was still—still as death itself, she thought; and yet the surging and noise in her ears went on. Once she thought Will was calling to her, "Dym, Dym, my dear!" She slid on to her knees and gasped for breath when she heard that, and holding her hands tightly over her burning forehead, whispered out a prayer that God would be good to her and give her strength to see Will again.

She felt better after that, and turned the handle of the parlour door. Some vague instinct told her she should find him there, sitting with clasped hands and smiling white face, as she had seen him last, and she stood stupefied and dizzy for a moment, looking round the dark empty room, till the gleam of light from under the folding-doors recalled her.

They had taken him away; he would look different, somehow. She had scarcely strength to push the door open now; the lights, the whiteness, the awful straightness of the dim form under the sheet, the paraphernalia of the death-chamber, seemed to freeze her faculties and turn her into stone.

How long she would have stood there she never knew, only a little hunched-up figure, sitting at the foot of the bed, slowly shuffled round to her and slid a soft little hand in hers.

"Don't be afraid; there is nothing to be afraid of, father says. Come and look at him; he is smiling like one of God's dear angels he used to tell us about;" and Dick drew her forward, and folded back the white covering.

"Smiling like one of God's dear angels." Thanks, little Dick, for those brave words. Now the hot pain beats less fiercely in her temples; tears that bring their own healing blot out the dear face again and again.

"Would you deprive me of such a welcome as that?" he had said to her. Ah, no need to question that welcome now! The furrows of pain had smoothed out of that calm brow; peace unutterable, profound, yet full of mystery, lay on the closely-folded lips and on the white carved face. There he lay, the young soldier of the Cross, called out from the battle in the very burden and heat of the day. Some one had crossed the meek arms over his breast, and laid a cluster of leaves and spring flowers within the hands; one of these had got loosened and disarranged. Dym picked it up, and placed it carefully back again—it was a green rowan spray.

On the day of the funeral they brought her his Bible, his gold cross and pocket-book, and a lock of soft fair hair that Susan had cut off when he lay in his coffin.

Dym was forced to own herself ill now: a strange fever and helplessness were upon her. Since the night when they had found her lying with her face hidden on the dead man's breast, and her arms clasped so tightly round his neck that they had some trouble to loosen them, and had carried her back to her little bed, she had never seen him again.

Sometimes in the night a sort of delirium came on, and she would try to go down and seek him. Little Dick saw her once standing with loosened hair and shining eyes in the middle of her room, her body swaying to and fro from weakness.

"Come, let us go to him," she said, holding out a hot hand to the boy. "What was that you said, Dick?—'Smiling like one of God's dear angels'—yes, I remember. We shall not waken him, Dick, none of us; I only want to sit beside him and look at him again."

Dick called his mother, and they laid her down again. "Not to-night, dearie; you must not try to-night." And Dym would cry out in a bitter voice, " They are keeping me from you, Will. O Will, your poor little Dym—your poor little unhappy Dym !" and her hands would beat the air weakly. Sometimes she would be quieter, and let Susan hush her to sleep; the fond woman would rock the girl's head on her bosom till drowsiness overpowered her grief. Dym would moan out fragments of talk. Once she thought she was in her brother's arms again.

"O Will, I do love you—I do love you so!" she said, pressing Susan's rough hands closer to her. Her cheeks were wet with tears when she awoke, but her face had a more peaceful expression on it.

It was the day of the funeral, but they did not dare to tell her so till afterwards; the dog sat whining on her bed half the day, and once he took hold of her sleeve and tried to drag her with his teeth. Dym was too dull and sick to notice the animal's restlessness; she lay torpid and half asleep, unmindful of the unusual sounds about the house.

Little Dick came in once with his eyes swollen with crying. He had just come home with his father, and had hung his linnet's cage with black. Dym heard the bird's chirping in a dismal sort of way, under the veil of premature night.

Richard Maynard had followed, and so had many of the parishioners. The old vicar of St. Jude's had read the service. Quite a crowd of women and children had followed the poor priest to his resting-place. Some navvies to whom he had done a kindness and the elder lads from the night-schools carried the bier. Not one of the friends he loved stood beside his grave, and yet there were no lack of mourners—the children he had baptized followed hand-in-hand, and flung little garlands of simple grasses and field flowers on the coffin as it was lowered from their sight; the tears ran down many a woman's face; the men and boys dragged rough sleeves across their eyes. "He was the poor man's priest; we shall never get such another," said one of them; and a woman who heard it answered, "Ay, but he was too good for the likes of us; it is the best that is taken; there is not one of us women that haven't lost a friend."

Dym never spoke when they told her, only she turned very white; she clutched the things they brought her and held them tight; that little worn Bible was dearer to her than anything else, except the lock of soft hair. Dym slept that night holding them still.

It was some days before she ventured to open the pocket-book. There were only a few simple memoranda, money accounts, a visiting-list, addresses of parishioners who had lately moved; there was nothing but the dear handwriting to make it valuable.

Dym was closing it carefully when a little folded paper dropped out of one of the pockets. She opened it; there was a withered flower—pressed carefully—and under it, in Will's handwriting, "Given to me by Honor, on her wedding-day, May —, 185—. *Qui patitur vincit.*"

Why does Dym suddenly flush up, and press the flower hurriedly to her lips and bosom? Why does she call out Will's name, in those troubled loving tones, as she kindles a light, and watches as the paper and its enclosure crackles into ashes? Has she found out his secret?

"It is all safe with me, dear; no one shall know. O Will! my darling—my darling, to think of this!" And then she whispered softly through her tears, as though he could hear her, that it is so brave to die and make no sign; that she loved him all the dearer for it; that he was her own Will Conqueror still!

Ay, Conqueror; and how nobly she will never know. *Qui patitur vincit.*

## CHAPTER V.

### "SOME DAYS MUST BE DARK AND DREARY."

AND so the weeks go on. Dym sickens and gets well, and broods silently over her sorrow, and spends long hours sitting in Will's chair with the little worn Bible in her lap, fingering the pages, but never reading, and looking with heavy lustreless eyes at the blazing streets outside. How long has she sat there?

It is June sunshine now, they tell her; the flower-girls hold up bunches of roses and carnations as they pass. Will's plants droop their heads thirstily as Dick waters them; the linnets flutter and chirp in the hot area below; Kiddle-a-wink basks on a bit of sunny pavement, and the splash of water from Susan's washing-tub seems to drip endlessly on the flags outside; but nothing rouses Dym from her listlessness, or from that dreary fingering.

Friends came about her in her trouble. Anna von Freiligrath sits in the little parlour for hours, turning the heel of a huge grey stocking, and chattering kind little commonplaces. Anna clasped her in her sturdy arms, and positively wept over her, when Dym came in in her black dress with her passive white face. "*Ach Himmmel!* how thou art changed, *mien Liebling!*" she bursts out with a little effusion of grief and sympathy; but Anna can make nothing of her, neither can Mrs. Tressilian when she drives up in her fine carriage and tries to take Dym away with her. Dym thanks them all, they are very good to her, but she would rather stay where she is; she is not lonely, she tells them; she has Susan, and little Dick, and Kiddle-a-wink; there is nothing she wants except—and here she breaks off and covers her face with her hand, and the tears splash down on her black dress—she only wants to be alone with him, so she sobs out, only alone with him.

"But you will make yourself ill, my child," says Mrs. Tressilian with motherly tones; she is quite moved from her usual apathy. "Mrs. Maynard, my good creature, she will make herself sick again if she stops in this close room. What will my sister say, and all of them? And I have promised to look after her!"

"Oh, no, no! leave me with Susan; Susan will take care of me," returned the girl, wrapping the homely arms round her. When Mrs. Tressilian had driven away, she put up her hand and stroked Susan's face.

"You will take me to see it to-day, dear, wont you? I am sure I am strong enough now." And Susan, who has not the heart to refuse her anything, consents after a little demur.

Dym ties on her bonnet wearily, and they go out into the sunshine, and Dick goes with them

—Dick, whose little face grows every day paler and more shrunken, but who never complains that his crutches are too heavy for him, or that he coughs and catches his breath oddly at night. The people look after the girl as she passes along the streets with her homely companions. Something in the stricken white face, in the soft dark eyes, in the air of refinement that pervades her, seems to attract them. Dick shoulders his crutch and puts back his cap in quite a manful manner, as he hobbles along by Dym's side.

"You will be sure to like it, it is so pretty; full of green trees and white crosses, and with little flower-beds where the children are; he used to like it too, he told me so;" and Dick hunched his shoulders and winked away a tear or two.

Yes, Dym liked it; once she and Will had walked there, and he had pointed out a little corner which he said was his favourite corner. There was a little clump of trees and a seat, and a tiny lawn with a sweetbriar hedge; one or two children's graves were near it. They had laid him not far from this place. The wind had strewn some rose-leaves over the grass mound; a garland hung half withered on the slim cross. Anna Freiligrath and Edith had put it there; there was a little basket of roses and fresh moss lying on the turf. How quiet and sweet it was! Roses were blooming, green trees waved, a gleam of white crosses shone in the sunshine; overhead was a tender blue sky, birds were singing, more garlands waving. Some children came up with a pot of arum lilies, and looked pitifully at the girl sitting in the grass with the crippled boy beside her.

"I am glad we came here, very glad," she said when the sun had set, and Susan had spoken some word as to the lateness of the hour. She would have sat on there till nightfall, with her cheek resting against the soft turf; but at Susan's gentle hint she rose at once.

"Good-bye, dear. I shall come again; it has done me good," Dick heard her whisper. She looked back once as the great gates swung on them: there lay the still garden, God's acre, as it is fitly called; through the trees shone a radiance and golden glory of clouds; the sun was sinking behind the little chapel; a pale crescent moon rose in the evening blue; a rose-laden wind blew across the dewy lawns; the paths had a white glitter of their own; a stone angel drooped its wings under an acacia-tree—some one had laid a great white lily at its feet. The gate clanged after them; before them was a dusty interminable road, people coming and going, whips cracking, jaded horses coming up the hill, a great red sun dazzling in the west.

"I am glad I came," says Dym, looking out before her with grave unseeing eyes; "it has taken a little of the pain away to see it so quiet and restful. Do you know the words that kept recurring to my mind all the time?—'Let us go, that we may die with him.' O Susan, I did so long to lie down and have done with it all!"

"You mustn't feel that, dearie."

"See how far that milestone is from us: we seem scarcely to move, and yet I suppose we shall reach it some time. How long is it since— since I came to you that Saturday?"

"A month to-day—Richard was only saying so this morning."

"A month—only four slow weeks? O Susan, to think I am not twenty yet, and that I am longing to have done with it all!"

"There is the milestone," breaks in Dick, with a child's literal interpretation of facts.

"But it is not my milestone, Dick," replies Dym, with a curious sad smile. How will she ever make them understand the sick loathing that has come upon her? Is she "a shadow in a world of shadows?" Are those really living people, with flesh and blood, with pains and aches and smiling faces, coming towards them out of the sunshine? Have any of them left a brother lying out on the hill yonder? When she is old and withered, will her heart wither too—will she cease to suffer? How long will she have to go on like this, with only Susan and little Dick for her companions—a month only? Have they forgotten her at Mentone? Mrs. Chichester has only written once—a hurried shocked letter, brimming over with sympathy, and begging Dym to put herself under Mrs. Tressilian's care. Dym had read it languidly, but it never came into her mind to answer it. "These are sad days with us all, and I have nothing comforting to say about my son, only the poor baby thrives "—that was all Mrs. Chichester wrote. He was too ill to send her a message, then; probably they had not yet told him he had lost his friend. There was no mention of Humphrey at all. That letter, loving as it was, added a still keener pang to the girl's pain as she read it. No, she could not write—not yet, at least. Presently, when she was stronger, and could bear to speak of her troubles.

But Dym was thinking of them all as she walked along, with one hand holding up her black dress and the other grasping the withered garland.

Dick was dragging himself wearily along on his crutches; Dym's gown dropped by-and-bye, and trailed in the grey dust. A clock struck; a church-bell sounded in the distance; the streets were full of children, as usual—of shrill young voice, of dissonant tones; the women sat working on their doorsteps; the monastery chimes rang out from the brown straggling building in Maitland Park. Are these monks real monks, with sandalled feet and shorn heads, Dym wonders? A little thin Sister of Mercy, with fluttering veil and dusty cloak, comes round the corner; a pair of smiling eyes look at her out of a wrinkled pale face; the bell ceases, and the little Sister goes on quicker, with hurried toddling steps. Dym thinks she would like to be a Sister; a sudden memory comes across her of a convent-garden she has once seen.

The bell is ringing out for vespers. There is

a straight long lawn and tall lilies; the nuns come down a lime-walk; there is a sudden shadowy gleam of black and white; the sun is setting behind a low grey building, with a passion-flower climbing round a porch; upstairs there are more lilies; a shining altar; low chanting; down the whitewashed passages come more black-and-white figures, and pass into the fragrant chapel. Well, there are places here, scores of them, for empty lives and open yearning hands. Dym thinks, with a sudden heart-ache, that she is not good enough, as she goes slowly up the steps.

Susan says her dear young lady is very tired and must lie down a little, but Dym shakes her head. There is not a speck of colour in her face. As she enters the shadowy little parlour, somebody, standing with his back to the light, starts forward with an exclamation as the dusty little figure comes wearily in—

"Miss Elliott! O my poor child!"

Dym gives a great sob when she sees Humphrey's honest face. They have not forgotten her then. The little room seems brightened somehow as those kindly eyes greet her in the twilight, as the rugged brown hand stretches itself out. Dym holds it for a moment between both of hers.

"O Humphrey, dear good Humphrey, you have come to me!"

"They sent me; I wanted to come. I am so glad, if you think I shall be of any use to you."

Humphrey can hardly frame his clumsy sentences as those little hands clutch hold of his coat-sleeve. He can scarcely bear to look at the small white face and troubled eyes brimming over with tears.

"I do not know whether you can be of any use to me, but I am glad you have come."

Dym's gladness threatened to become hysterical; she almost clung to the kind friend who had come all these miles to find her in her trouble.

"O Humphrey, it is such terrible loneliness; but I know you will be good to me," she said, looking at him in a pitiful childish way.

Humphrey had need of all his fortitude before he could apply himself to soothe her.

"I will do my best for you; you know that, Dym," he said, looking at her with mournful eyes.

Humphrey seemed older than ever in his black clothes. His forehead was deeply lined, and the hard-featured face had a sallow tint on it. No wonder, after what he had gone through, that Humphrey looked almost ill. The faithful creature had travelled night and day ever since they had given him leave to seek her.

"I don't know whether she will be glad to see me, but I feel I ought to go," he had said to Mrs. Chichester; "she may be ill, or wanting something."

"Perhaps she may have gone to Celia's. Do you think Guy can spare you?" answered the poor mother doubtfully.

7—2

But her words, low as they were, reached her son's ears.

"Let him go, mother; he ought to go. There is nothing that he or anyone else can do for me; it is different with her."

And Guy Chichester walked up and down the long room with fierce impatient strides, as he had walked night and day, his mother thought, as she listened to those never-ending footsteps.

So Humphrey had gone without sleep, taking it by snatches, and had travelled back through the weary miles, hardly daring to expect a welcome. But he never forgot to his dying day the quiver of light that came over the weary face as Dym ran up to him with outstretched hands, and called him "her dear good Humphrey."

She laid aside her bonnet now, with its dusty crape trimmings. Humphrey watched her hurriedly smoothing her soft hair with her hands and straightening the little frill round her neck.

"See who has come to me, Susan," she said, turning round with a sad smile as Mrs. Maynard came in. "They have not forgotten me; they have sent him."

And the girl laid her head on Susan's shoulder and cried a little, out of sheer oppression of thankfulness. Will would be glad Humphrey had come to her, she thought. Humphrey's eyes had a dumb hungry look in them as the tears streamed over the sweet face. Susan might pet and comfort her, but he could only stand aloof and make useless offers of help. Humphrey was growing sad again, when Dym suddenly held out her hand to him, as though to entreat his forgiveness.

"I cannot help it, Humphrey, it has been such pain; and now I don't feel quite so terribly lonely. You will tell me all about them presently, will you not?" And then she brushed her tears away, and busied herself in helping Susan to prepare the meal for the tired traveller.

Humphrey protested that he did not need either meat or drink; but Dym would not believe him. When Susan lighted the lamp, she drew the easy-chair to the table, and pressed the viands on him with trembling eagerness. Humphrey wanted to wait on her instead.

"Do let me. If you know what it is to have some one of whom to take care again—I have missed that more than all. I—he——"

Humphrey nearly choked over his first morsel, as Dym buried her head on her hands and sobbed.

She hurried away after that, and had it out by herself. These sick longings would come upon her suddenly. "O Will, I shall never take care of you again. You don't want me now," she would say at such times.

She came back with the same worn gentle look, and sat down by Humphrey. "Now you will tell me," she said in a low voice. "I want to hear everything—everything."

"There is not much to tell," Humphrey says.

He goes over the sad story as curtly as he dare, and yet he feels an odd relief in telling it.

Dym did not interrupt, except by a question or two. She sat leaning forward, with her cheek on her hand, and her eyes fixed on Humphrey's face. Sometimes a tear rolled down, and she forgot to wipe it away. That fixed sad gaze made it difficult to Humphrey to go on; now and then he faltered and almost broke down.

"How did it happen?" Dym asked; "at the baptism?"

"Yes, she took cold then," Humphrey answered; "some one had left a door or window open—the nurse, he believed. She was sitting up, and over-excited or fatigued. Guy noticed her shiver when he came in and put the baby in her arms; but she said it was nothing, and he forgot it afterwards. The clergyman and his wife came in and talked to her, and after a time she had seemed very tired. Guy lifted her back to bed again; but she did not feel inclined to sleep. When the doctor came in he found her still talking, with two spots of colour in her cheeks, and her eyes shining like grey stars, and had scolded them both. Honor had pleaded that the baby might be left with her; but he had sternly ordered it away. 'We must have no more excitement; you must go to sleep,' he said quite angrily; and then he muttered something about the want of common sense in people.

"Honor gave a quaint little smile when she was left alone.

"'I did want baby so,' Guy heard her say. The grey eyes would not close; they were smiling wide open at Guy as he leant over her some time afterwards, and then again he noticed the shiver.

"But still he was not alarmed," Humphrey

said, "and retired to bed as happy as usual; but towards morning they had called him. The doctor must be sent for, they told him in frightened voices; she was very uneasy, and in great pain, but had begged them not to wake him before.

"Guy rushed into his wife's room. She was evidently in great suffering. There was a troubled —almost scared—look in her eyes; but they grew calm when she saw him.

"'Come here, Guy; nurse says I have taken cold. Can it be that that is the matter with me? I feel so strange.'

"Guy strove to hide the anguish that assailed him; he took her in his arms and soothed and comforted her. They say the dear beautiful smile came to her lips every time she looked at him," added Humphrey in a choked voice.

"But, alas, sharp inflammation had set in, and for a short hour she knew no one. 'Where is our little child? Where is our baby, Guy?' she kept asking; and then she went murmuring on in disconnected sentences about broken crystals, and white robes, and cleansing waters. 'They have washed my baby quite clean,' she kept saying. 'The cross was all bubbles and brightness; I saw it sparkle. Don't let any one kiss the water away—my little Florence—my own baby.'

"She seemed sinking into a lethargy at last, and some one said she was going. The words seemed to rouse her, for she opened her eyes full on her husband's heart-broken face.

"'O Guy, is it that?' they heard her whisper; 'not that, husband?'

"'My darling, I fear so.'

"'Must I leave you and baby?' and as, unable to speak, he supported her on his breast, she made a sign that he should kiss her.

"'Oh, it has been so beautiful!' Those were the last words that those standing round her could catch; but Guy, bending his ear to her lip, heard a faint sigh, 'Not my will;' and then somebody came behind him and laid her down."

Dym's face was hidden now, and there was a long silence.

"How did he bear it?" she asked at last, almost in a whisper.

Humphrey shook his head sorrowfully.

"He has not borne it; he has fought against it so, that for the first three weeks we almost thought he would lose his reason. He says such things that his mother goes out of the room shuddering; but he is quieter now."

"Has he been ill?"

"Mentally ill of course; he sleeps badly, and wakes in a strong fever. He is beginning to look haggard and grey; no one can do anything with him—his mother least of all."

"Poor Mrs. Chichester!"

"Madam does her best, to give her her due. She bears his fierce humours as an angel would; but her tears anger him. Once or twice she brought the baby to him—poor lady, she knew no better; but he just flung away, and shut himself up for nearly twenty-four hours at a stretch."

"O Humphrey, is it possible that he does not care for his child?"

"It is too early days to talk of that now, poor little lamb; she will grow into his heart by-and-bye. They say she has Honor's eyes. You see he has got it into his head that the babe has cost her her life; he has never taken her into his arms since."

"I can understand just how he feels."

"But he looks at her sometimes when he thinks no one sees him. I saw him once standing by her cot, with his arms folded over his chest. 'Our little child,' I heard him mutter—'yes, she said that—will she grow up an angel too? O baby, I think I should kill myself—I should, I must, to get rid of all this misery—if it were not for the fear I should not see her again;' and then his head fell forward on his arms with such a groan, and he let me lead him away. I stopped with him all night. Somehow I did not dare to leave him alone."

"O Humphrey, you ought not to have left him now."

"How could I help it?" stammered Humphrey; "he sent me. I have promised to go back again, if Madam wants me. She wont leave him just yet; but I can't help thinking he will break away from us altogether soon. He gave Madam such a look when she ventured to suggest his coming back to Ingleside."

Dym gave a heavy sigh. He would go away from them all. "He will come back, my girl; I know him so well: these noble souls are not left to wander away in outer darkness." Ah, she could almost hear Will say these words! How often in the months, nay, years to come, she recalled them with a strange feeling of comfort! through what dreary experiences was their Sintram passing, while the mother prayed Verena-like through her tears—the mother on earth and the wife in paradise weaving the twofold cord that was to bring him home again!

Humphrey went away as soon as his sad story was finished. Dym made him promise to come again early the next day; he should take her to St. Luke's, she thought. When the morning came she sat in her old place beside him, with her heavy crape veil falling over her face; the lilac sunshine was flooding the chancel again; outside the poplars waved. A stranger knelt in Will's place.

"Are you sure this has been good for you?" asked Humphrey, somewhat conscience-stricken, as the girl put back her veil and looked at him.

Dym had dark circles round her eyes; but a gentle light shone from under the reddened eyelids.

"I could hear his voice all through; we had his favourite Psalms to-day. You were very good to take me, Humphrey," pressing his arm softly.

Dym made him take her somewhere else, too. Her tongue loosened as she sat on the grass beside Will's grave, fingering the daisies lovingly: she poured out the whole history of her trouble into Humphrey's ears as he stood beside her.

"Ay, ay, poor child, poor child!"

Humphrey did not say much more, though

his honest heart was overflowing with sympathy. Yet Dym thought his kindness was perfect.

Humphrey had yielded himself quite submissively to the girl's will throughout the day; but on the following morning things were otherwise.

"I ought to have given you this before," he said, somewhat abruptly, producing a letter from his pocket. Dym was dusting and straightening Will's books, and a volume of Hooker dropped from her fingers as she caught sight of Mrs. Chichester's handwriting.

"Madam wrote it in a hurry," continued Humphrey, thrusting his hands into his shooting-coat, and assuming an indifference he did not feel; "she hopes you will decide on remaining at her sister's till her return, as it will be so lonely for you at Ingleside."

"She has given me my choice," returned Dym disconsolately. "Oh, why, why will they not leave me alone? Write to her, Humphrey; tell her I am happier here."

"Nay, nay, you must not ask me to do that," returned Humphrey, puckering up his brow with the air of a man who has a tough job before him; "you'll only fret out your heart stopping on here, and turning over his things all day long, as Mrs. Maynard says you have been doing. Come," he added coaxingly, "you will be a good child and go to Mrs. Tressilian's."

"I cannot," replied Dym, bursting into tears. "Why is every one so cruel? Mrs. Chichester does not want me—nobody wants me!" with a little outburst of impatience and despair that goes to Humphrey's heart; but he steels his tenderness and answers her very gravely.

"You ought not to have said that to me; but you did not know what you were saying, did you, my dear? You are so young that you cannot judge for yourself in this; you must let me decide for you, as though I were your—your brother," stammered out poor Humphrey, not thinking how bitterly the word would sound to the bereaved girl.

"No, you can never be that. I have no brother but Will—no one but Will. O my darling, to think you will never help me to be good again!"

Humphrey had to wait till the girl's grief had spent itself a little, and then he returned to the subject very gently but firmly.

"I wish you had some one better to advise you," he said very sadly; "but I will not go away and leave you like this. Madam is right— you are not fit to take care of yourself."

"Susan will take care of me. O Humphrey, why will you be so hard on me? I would be so good if you will only let me stop here."

But Humphrey shook his head.

"It cannot be done. I have passed my word to put you under Mrs. Tressilian's protection, or to see you safe at Ingleside."

Humphrey's manner has a trifle of austerity in it, all the more that he feels his resolution melting.

"I will go to Ingleside then," returned Dym in a low voice.

She was a little scared at Humphrey's peremptoriness; she turned paler, and her head drooped on her breast as Humphrey quietly told her that she must prepare to go back with him on the morrow.

"I have my work to see after: everything is at a standstill; the home-farm is without a bailiff," finished Humphrey apologetically.

But Dym turned away from him. He had been hard to her; he would not write and ask permission for her to stay; every one treated her like a child, Humphrey worst of all, though he loved her. Dym went away in a little fury of despair, leaving poor Humphrey crestfallen over his victory.

It was a miserable day for every one. Humphrey wandered about the streets, and came back again to find Dym quietly crying over her work, with Susan helping her; through the half-opened door he could see the little black figure kneeling before a pile of clothes and books; Dick was standing by; Susan seemed to be expostulating.

"I wouldn't do it, dearie; leave them for Richard and me to manage; it doesn't seem right; it is morbid-like, and unchristian."

"These are the shirts I made for him, Susan; and look at that poor old coat with the rent under the arm. I usen't to like to see him in it, but he never would part with it—never. Fold it up carefully, Susan, with the others. I tell you I must take them."

Susan sighed and shook her head. In another moment there was a heavy stride in the next room, and the folding-door was pushed open.

"Give that to me, please, Mrs. Maynard; that and the others. I will not have it done." Humphrey spoke quite sternly, and there was a frown on his face. "You ought not to allow Miss Elliott to do things that are bad for her—you, who are her friend, should know better than that."

"She wont mind us, sir; one can't be hard on the poor lamb," said Susan in a disturbed voice.

"Humphrey, go away; you have no right to interfere with me!" exclaimed the poor child, putting out a feverish hand to stop him; but Humphrey took hold of it, and suddenly lifted her up.

"I will not have it done," he repeated firmly. "You are wearing yourself out, and you have no one to take care of you. You must not move till I give you leave." And to Dym's infinite amazement she found herself placed on the couch, and covered with Humphrey's rug.

"Susan and I will pack the books," was all he said as he went out of the room. Dym lay looking after him in a curious sort of way. He had taken the things from her hand, and had thrown them aside; he had put her out of the way, as though she had been a mere infant; and yet she was not angry; she had never liked him better than when he had stood by her with a frown on his face, and then had tenderly stooped and lifted her in his strong arms. There was something healing in the rough tenderness that had interposed between her and that weary labour.

I think, if Humphrey Nethecote had been another sort of man, he might almost have won Dym at this time. The girl was so lonely and unhappy that she would have clung to any strong arm that had offered itself for her support. In the months that followed she felt for him a quiet tenderness, which might have ripened into love, if he had only been less humble with her, and had shown her the more dominant side of his character. Dym could not love where she did not reverence strongly. Humphrey was good, kindness itself, as she assured herself over and over again; but there was something wanting. His great love made him timid and self-deprecating.

Once, many months afterwards, when a sort of dry fever of hoplessness came over the girl—when there seemed nothing left to live for, and only the dull level of existence lay before her—a sudden impulse came into her mind that she would make this man happy who had loved her and served her so faithfully.

It was one of those perilous thoughts that sometimes come into a girl's mind, and might have worked her mighty woe in the years to come, if Humphrey's generosity had not saved them both.

She had said some word that the man could hardly mistake, and Humphrey had looked at her incredulously for a moment, and then a sudden tinge of red had come into his sallow face.

"Do you mean this, my dear?"

"Yes, I think so," Dym replied, looking at the strong homely features, working with emotion; but her voice had a fixed weary tone in it. "Everything is very miserable, but I should like to make you happy, Humphrey."

"God bless you!" was all he said for a moment. But as he took her in his arms a shiver passed over her, for she thought he had taken her at her word; but she need not have feared him.

"I will try to be good to you," she whispered; but there was a chill sick feeling at her heart, that ought to have warned her.

"You are always good to me; don't be afraid. I shall never forget this—never; but you must not come to me; you do not love me, my dear."

"Not much—not in that way," she stammered, crimsoning under that honest gaze; "but I thought it would be nice to make you happy."

"You would not make me happy; don't you understand we should both be miserable?—unless you cared for me."

"I shall love you all the more dearly for this," as Dym shrank away from him almost timidly; "but no man ought to marry a woman who does not love him."

Humphrey was quite hot and dusty when he came up to Dym's couch in the late afternoon.

"We have finished; Maynard is cording the boxes. You must not be angry with me, Miss

Elliott, because I have taken this into my own hands."

"I am not angry," said Dym, slipping her hand into his with a sweet smile. "Why do you call me Miss Elliott? I am very much obliged to you, Humphrey; it is I who have been wrong. I ought not to have given you so much trouble."

Humphrey was quite taken aback by the girl's humility and gentleness.

Humphrey had no more trouble with her after that; next morning she took leave of her humble friends, and was very quiet and dry-eyed when he put her into the carriage. Little Dick climbed up for a last embrace, and Susan had her apron up to her eyes.

"Good-bye; you have all been so good to me," faltered Dym.

The sun streamed down on the dusty pavement; the women came to their doors and looked after the retreating carriage. Dym, leaning back and closing her eyes, saw a quiet face with an ineffable smile stamped upon it, and knew that wherever she went, that one day she should see it again, "smiling at her like one of God's dear angels."

Dym was too weary to say much to Humphrey when he parted from her at the door of Ingleside. The servants went downstairs and spoke pityingly of the young creature who looked so changed and pale in her deep mourning; even Mrs. Fortescue melted at the sight of the sad young face, and kissed her quite affectionately.

Dym, who was yearning for love and sympathy, never forgot that kiss.

Dym would have been puzzled if any one had asked her how she spent her days. Humphrey came often, but he did not stay long; and by-and-bye he went back to Mentone. Mr. Chichester had been seized with a low fever, which prolonged their stay; but as soon as he was able to bear the fatigue, Humphrey went to remove them to a cooler place; and by slow stages and frequent pauses he hoped to bring them safely to England by the middle of August.

Dym wrote long letters to Mrs. Chichester, and took endless walks with Kiddle-a-wink, and grew more miserable every day; she was longing for her friends—pining for them; and the delay grew more sickening each hour.

"We are coming home," wrote Humphrey at last to her, and Dym's heart gave a sudden bound; but as she read the next few words it sank lower and lower; "if all be well we shall be with you in another forty-eight hours—that is, Madam and the nurse and baby; but the Squire has suddenly made up his mind to take a sea-voyage—he talks of going out by one of the Peninsular and Oriental steamers to Calcutta.

"He has shaken off the effects of his illness, but looks languid still. I think, for Madam's sake, it is a pity that the doctors have put this notion of a sea-voyage into his head, for if he once get away from us, one can never know when he will come back again. I think it is better to face trouble than to run away from it, as he has done all his life," finished Humphrey in his blunt way.

As Dym opened this letter a note dropped out and fell to the ground. Dym's hand fairly shook as she picked it up, and the colour rushed to her face, for she recognised Mr. Chichester's handwriting.

"MY DEAR MISS ELLIOTT,—Perhaps you have thought that I might have written before; but what is there that we can find to say to each other? There is only one person to whom, in all these four months, I could have borne to have spoken of my trouble, and that is your brother, and he is dead. Had he lived, I might have spent a lifetime at St. Luke's, trying to work out some of my misery, instead of vainly endeavouring to crush it out in miles of ocean. So you have lost him! I am grieved still more in my grief to know it; but be comforted, you are too young to break your heart, and life has something in reserve for *you*. I am sending my mother and child home to Ingleside. I know you will love and take care of them. Be my faithful little friend, still, and help my mother to forget some of her cares.

"God bless you! When you have a prayer to spare you may waste it on one who is ever your true friend,

"GUY LATIMER CHICHESTER."

It was that letter, so curt, so tender, yet so bitter in its sorrow, that first roused Dym from the apathy of her own grief.

The harvest-fields were being reaped round Birstwith when Mrs. Chichester bade farewell to her son, and came back to her solitary home, escorted by the faithful Humphrey.

Dym ran out on the sunny terrace to receive them, and just in time to see Humphrey assisting the foreign-looking nurse to descend from the carriage.

Dym stretched out her arms when she caught sight of the fluttering white cloak and dimpled hands. "Oh, give me the baby!" she cried; and as she stooped over it the child opened a pair of solemn grey eyes and smiled at her.

"Little Florence, little Florence, how I shall love you!" whispered Dym; and for the first time since Will's death something like returning happiness stole into her face.

## CHAPTER VI.

### "ALL IN THE WILD MARCH MORNING."

THREE years and a half have passed away since the events recorded in the last chapter—more than three whole years since Guy Chichester took his passage in the *Montezuma en route* for Calcutta; and still Ingleside is without its master.

It is more than eighteen months now since they have heard from him.

And some who loved him well say that the brief unhappy life is finished, and that Guy Chichester will never come back to his own again.

Mr. Fortescue says so, and Cousin Katherine; and Humphrey even shakes his honest head more sadly every day when the Squire's name is mentioned; and Beatrix Delaire puts on mourning, and cries her beautiful eyes quite dim for the cousin she has lost; but still the mother hopes and prays, and stretches out her arms to Dym when she comes in to wish her a grave good-night.

"What was it he said? tell me again, my dear;" and Dym whispers the words, which have become a part of her creed: "He will come back, my girl; I know him so well: these noble souls are not left to wander away in outer darkness." And as Mrs. Chichester kisses her, and calls her her comforter, Dym's lip trembles, and her eyes fill with tears, for she knows that, whether he is dead or alive, the mother will never look upon her son's face again.

Mrs. Chichester has wept herself blind again.

"God bless dear papa, and bring him home to Flossie and gran'ma," lisps little Florence, night after night, at Dym's knee; and in the morning, when the solemn grey eyes open, she wakes Dym to ask, "Has papa come back yet?"

Florence knows her father's face by heart; she kisses it every night when she says her prayers. "Papa isn't pretty, like mamma or auntie," thinks Flossie; she likes mamma's face best. A tender image of that sweet mother is already enshrined in the child's mind, a faint glory of shining raiment and white wings and smiling eyes, like the angel she sees at church. On Sunday evenings Dym takes her on her lap, and tells her about that loving guardianship; she talks about her father on other evenings; but on these quiet Sabbath hours she speaks of Honor to Honor's child.

She and Florence exchanged confidences. Dym has quaint sweet theories of her own: it is to her an article of faith that Honor is watching over her little daughter. Florence is not quite sure about the wings—does Auntie know? A grand beautiful lady, all in white, kissed her last night; Florence could see the stars shining round her head.

"Perhaps papa will come to-night," finishes Florence sleepily; "but I like mamma's kisses best, only I think she was crying, for my face was quite wet in the morning." Dym holds her peace: she would not have told Florence for worlds that it was only a dream; that it was her kisses and tears that the child felt, when Dym was saying her prayers beside her in the moonlight.

Dym thinks of little Florence when she reads Nathan's story of the ewe-lamb; for three years, ever since her foster-mother left the ten-months' old babe, Honor's child has slept in her bosom, and grown into her heart of hearts.

Dym does not know what she would have done all these years without the child! ever since the long illness through which she nursed her, and which threatened to extinguish the precious little life, Florence had seemed to belong to her more than to any one else. "They tell me her own mother could not have done more for her," wrote Guy Chichester in one of those rare letters of his. "Heaven reward you for all your goodness to me and mine!"

Dym carried that letter about with her wherever she went. It was more than eighteen months since she received it; he was coming home then. He was sick and weary of wandering, so he said, and was longing, with a feverish longing that surprised himself, to see the child that death had so nearly snatched away from him. "I think it is a punishment on my own hard-heartedness," he wrote; "I ought not to have stayed away so long from Honor's child."

What had he been doing with himself those two years? His letters made the two women giddy to read them: now he was tiger-hunting in the Indian jungles, now studying Hindostanee and teaching young natives in a missionary settlement; then he had made his way to Australia; when he last wrote, he had already taken his passage home in a vessel leaving Melbourne. It was the fate of that vessel, the *Rose and Crown*, that made Beatrix Delaire put on mourning for her cousin, and that dimmed the mother's eyes with anguish; for, hundreds of leagues from land, right out on the blue Pacific, the noble ship had caught fire, and nearly every soul on board had perished miserably. One boat's crew had indeed escaped, and two of the survivors, who had contrived after innumerable hardships to reach one of the coral-reef islands, had within the last few months been interrogated by Humphrey at Liverpool, and according to their account, Guy Chichester had been left in the burning vessel. One man there was indeed, who had manned the boat with his fierce energy, and without whom not one of all that boatful would have survived to tell the tale, but even he had succumbed to the exhaustion of thirst and fever. "We dropped him down as decently as we could, and one of us said a bit of a prayer over him; but we had hardly strength to pitch the others overboard. Dawson here says his name was Leicester or Latimer;" and Humphrey, wringing the poor fellow's hand, turned away without a word, for he thought, and others thought too, that that dominant spirit among the boat crew of despairing men was Guy Latimer Chichester. And Humphrey went up to Ingleside and told Dym—every one came to Dym now in their troubles; she was so gentle and helpful, she looked at them with such wistful kind eyes.

Dym was "Miss Elliott" still in the household, but Florence called her "Auntie." Uncle Humphrey had taught her to say it long ago, and Mrs. Chichester loved the name, for Dym was almost like her own daughter to the poor lady.

Dym shielded her face as she listened to Humphrey's story. Humphrey saw her shudder once, as though the strange coincidence of the name struck her; but when he had finished she uncovered her eyes and looked at him, and the lines of the mouth unbent slightly in their sweet gravity.

"Do you believe this was he, Humphrey?"

"Ay, surely; there can be no room for doubt, I fear."

"And you think he is lying miles below the Pacific; that he will never come home, never see his child again? We don't believe that, do we, Kelpie?" stooping to caress the faithful creature that seemed to have transferred his affection to her. "You and I and Will know better than that."

"Why do you hope against hope?" persisted Humphrey sadly. "I think you are wrong, Dym; I do indeed. It is false and cruel kindness to tell that poor woman her son is alive."

Humphrey spoke with unusual sternness, but his heart was very sore.

"If you withdraw that hope, she will die," returned Dym gently but firmly. "Promise me you will not tell her this, Humphrey—what the sailor said, I mean: you have no idea how weak she is; it would kill her."

"I wont go against you," returned Humphrey, looking at her wistfully from under his bent brows. "Where do you get your faith, Dym?"

Dym gave him a little smile in answer.

"You and I and Will know better than that," she repeated, kneeling on the rug and putting her arms round the dog's neck when Humphrey had gone; and the faithful collie licked her hand as though he understood her question.

Sad news had lately come to them from Lansdowne House. Colonel Delaire had met with an accident in the hunting-field, and Anna von Freiligrath wrote that serious consequences were apprehended. The doctors feared there was some internal mischief, and the invalid seemed to think so too, for he was calmly putting his affairs in order.

The news came to them at Christmas, and cast an additional gloom over the little party. Mrs. Chichester had been ailing for some time; lately the indisposition had increased, and the inclement season kept her a prisoner in her own room.

It was there that Dym read Fräulein von Freiligrath's sad letter.

Afterwards they watched for every post anxiously; but it was the middle of February before their worst fears were verified.

Colonel Delaire had borne his protracted sufferings heroically. A little before his death he had sent for his wife.

No one had thought the end was so near; and she came to his bedside dressed for an assembly, with diamonds shining on her white neck and arms. Some of her friends had persuaded her that her presence was indispensable at some gay gathering for an hour or two; and Beatrix, who found her husband's sick-room somewhat irksome, had yielded to their solicitations.

" You sent for me, Frank; do you feel worse ?" she asked a little anxiously. Perhaps she felt conscience-stricken.

" I think I do, my dear. I wanted to speak to you—that is if you can spare me a few minutes," he added, with a shade of bitterness in his voice that stung through all her worldliness and selfishness. There was unconscious irony in his words, but he had not meant to be hard on this woman, who had disappointed and blighted his life; he would die in peace with her and with all the world, he thought. He strove to forget that but for her he would have lived long happy years of usefulness; this marriage had broken his career and ruined his happiness; domestic misery had made him more reckless of his life than other men had been; he knew as they carried him home upon the stretcher that he had dared a useless leap to rouse himself from the sadness that preyed so continually upon him.

And yet how he had loved her! how her beauty had dazzled him!—it dazzled his dying eyes now; for the sake of that glorious face and form he had bartered the peace of his life; her beauty had been ashes and bitterness to him, and yet he loved her still.

No, he would not be hard on her; but one word he did say of sorrow and regret.

"It is all over with me, Beatrix. You might have been a little more patient, dear. I should not have troubled you long"—looking at her dress meaningly; it was his only reproach.

"I think we may as well say good-bye to each other," he went on. "We have not been happy together, it was more my fault than yours; I ought not to have made you marry me; you never loved me, Trichy; but it is too late to speak of that now."

"Yes, it was too late," thought Beatrix, as she stood beside him dry-eyed and speechless. She felt conscience-stricken and abashed before this simple kindly gentleman; she could not lie to him, she dare not affirm she had ever loved him. "Yes, it is too late to talk of that, Frank," she said, dragging the diamond bracelet on her arm, and not venturing to look at him.

Some hours later she stood there still shivering in her gay ball-dress. Some one noticed her shudder, and threw a cloak over her, but she shook her head and put it away with feverish fingers—she was not cold.

Guy Chichester thought he had tasted the bitterest dregs that pain could offer when Honor's arms dropped heavily about his neck; but even his misery was less intense than Beatrix's as she stood with hot dry eyes beside her husband's death-bed.

She did not venture to approach him; others, mere hirelings, pressed round him, and rendered him the necessary offices. Was it for her to touch him who had never loved him? who had neglected his sick-bed? whose forgiveness she had never asked or sought?

"Now, my men, for a last charge!" were his final words; and so the gallant soul stormed up the heights of death.

Dym generously forgot her old repugnance, and wrote to Beatrix in her trouble. There was still an unspoken antagonism between these two; but Beatrix was older now, a woman of the world, and she no longer showed her dislike openly to her aunt's companion; perhaps it was no longer safe to do so, for Dym's position at Ingleside was wholly unassailable. Even at Lansdowne House, and in her daughter's presence, Mrs. Tressilian petted and made much of her, and Beatrix had ceased to rebuke.

"You will all repent it one day," was the only speech she made to her mother. To Miss

Elliott she was perfectly civil; once or twice she had made some slight advance, but Dym had never cordially responded—to the end of her life she mistrusted Mrs. Delaire.

Dym's aptitude for nursing was greatly needed this winter. Mrs. Chichester did not rally from her indisposition; on the contrary, she grew weaker and weaker. Dr. Grey shook his head when he came out of the sick-room; there was no disease of which to speak, but a lamentable want of power, surprising in a woman of her constitution.

"There is no real wish to rally; this is purely inanition and a depressed state of the nerves," he said once quite impatiently to Dym, who had followed him downstairs. Humphrey, who was waiting in the hall to hear his report, joined them in the porch.

"That is what Miss Elliott says," he interrupted. "We cannot get Madam to take interest in anything; it is 'Do as you like, I am too tired to think,' from one week's end to the other."

"It must be checked," returned Dr. Grey decidedly. "There is no knowing what mischief may result when the patient is once allowed to sink into this state. She must be roused, interested in spite of herself, or there will be total collapse. The worst is, there is no remedy for the cause of all this; the only question is, whether any certainty would not be better than this state of hopeless suspense."

"That is what I say," put in Humphrey, with

a glance at Dym, who was standing by the fire smoothing her little silk apron thoughtfully.

Dym looked up quickly.

"No, no, Dr. Grey; don't let him say that; he is always telling me so. It would kill her; I am sure it would," speaking with her old energy.

"The question is whether she has really any hope remaining," returned Dr. Grey; "whether this indifference to everything does not mean that she has secretly relinquished it. Tell us, Miss Elliott—you are more with her than any one—do you think she believes her son is alive?"

"I don't know; she has not spoken of him lately," answered Dym in a low voice. "She has got all his things about her; her bed was quite strewn yesterday with broken toys and books, and even baby-clothes. Florence was telling her what everything was when I came in. I wanted to put them away, but she would not let me."

"She thinks that they are relics," returned Dr. Grey quickly. "I was right, you see; she never expects to have him back again."

"O Dr. Grey, I never thought of that," answered Dym, and the tears sprang to her eyes; "but indeed, indeed, you are mistaken. I remember now Florence was saying her prayers to her, and she made her say that part over twice about her father coming back."

Dr. Grey shook his head; he was quite of another opinion.

"If you take my advice, you will try to find out exactly what she thinks. I believe with

Mr. Nethcote that she knows already, and that she will be able to bear any certainty."

Dym was still standing by the fire when Humphrey came back from accompanying the doctor to the door. She turned to him with one of her worried looks.

"Humphrey, I can't bear this much longer—you all thinking me wrong, I mean; but some one else must tell her."

"Nay, surely no one understands her so well as you do, Dym."

"I cannot help that," with a touch of her old irritability; "if you and Dr. Grey persist in thinking it right, one of you must do it. It will not be a lie on your lips."

"Ay, whatever do you mean, Dym?"

"If I said he was dead, I should tell a lie; he is not dead—I feel it—I know it. What is the day of the month, Humphrey? I am beginning to forget everything;" and she put her hand to her head in a confused tired way.

"It is the twenty-first of March," returned Humphrey, looking at her in surprise; "Madam's been ailing over three months now. Let me see, Flo will be four years old on the twentieth of next month."

"Yes, yes, I know. I was not thinking of that. It is just three years and seven months, then, since he went away; a year and seven months since we last heard. It is a long time, a very long time, Humphrey; no wonder you all lose hope."

"The only marvel is you haven't lost it too,"

replied Humphrey in his gruffest tone; it made his heart ache to see how the girl clung to her belief; "but it is not any use; you will be obliged to let it go."

"Never! what are you talking about? I could not, I could not." Her eyes quite shone with excitement; her voice trembled and grew eager. "You may take away the last hope from that poor woman; I cannot prevent you—I dare not, if you think it right—but no one shall make me believe that he will not come back to his child one day."

Humphrey did not answer. Her earnestness staggered him in spite of himself. The Squire alive still? a year and seven months, and yet he had not reached them? The idea was too improbable; it was contrary to all reason. He would have liked to argue the girl out of her obstinate belief; but he feared angering her. Dym's fire was only a sudden blaze, and it died out as soon as Humphrey left her.

"They will reason me even out of this, if I listen to them. Why will they not leave me alone to believe what I like?" she said to herself, with a sudden spasm of doubt and misery. "Oh Kelpie, do you really think your master is dead—really, really dead?" But though the sagacious animal licked her hand in the same reassuring manner as before, she was not comforted.

Dym suddenly felt with a great terror that her hope was slipping from her. She had spoken bravely; but why did her heart all at once fail her? Was it that the suspense was becoming unbearable even to her? She had told Humphrey she would never believe he was dead; that it would be a lie on her lips if she said it to his mother. Why did her conscience accuse her of falseness? Had she meant what she said? Had she been utterly true? Had not her wish blinded her when she had so spoken?

Dym felt as though she were collapsing too; a sudden paralysis of fear was on her; her faith had received a shock in reality; the poor thing was weary and spent with nursing; fatigue and depression were wearing out her hopefulness. The body is often to blame for these moods. When Dym sat down with a little shiver and asked herself if she believed this thing or the other, she wanted to sleep away her fears.

It would have been a wonder if she had not been tired; she was too young and weak for such a responsibility; the strain of it was almost wearing her out.

Mrs. Chichester could hardly bear her to be out of the room. Dym schooled herself into brightness whenever she came near her friend. The poor invalid, in her blindness and helplessness, grew more dependent on her young companion every day. Dym's sweet voice never sounded tired in the sick-room; her light step—how it flagged when it crossed the threshold!—was like music to the ears that had grown to listen for it night and day; the soft touches that had once proved so soothing to Guy Chichester, were never weary of manipulating the hot brow. Dym kept untiring vigils in the sick-room; she denied herself needful rest, trying to beguile the tedium of those long nights. Mrs. Chichester never slept till dawn; for some hours she was always wakeful and restless. Dym had grown into the habit of taking the earliest part of the night-watch; Dorothy sat and dozed quite placidly all the rest of the time. Mrs. Chichester would be waiting for her now, she thought, with a touch of compunction at her idleness. Stewart came in to close the shutters as she rose wearily from her chair. "It is going to be a wild night, miss," he said, as Dym stood for a moment looking out at the black rain-clouds that were scudding across the sky. The wind was driving along the terrace and whistling fiercely among the gable-ends; the elms were creaking and straining their mighty limbs like angry giants; in the kitchen garden there was a flapping of bare boughs; that night the Nid was swollen, and lashed its banks with white froth. Later on the floodgates of heaven seemed open, and a driving rain and mist filled the valley; a hollow moaning reverberated among the hills, and echoed mournfully through the dim woods. Dym shivered as she passed the conservatory door, for it reminded her of that evening, more than three years ago, when Humphrey, with pale face and dripping clothes, stood in that very place and told her Honor was dead. Dym found Florence curled up among her grandmother's pillows when she entered the sick-room; the little maid had stolen across the corridor with her little white night-gown and bare rosy feet, and now sat open-eyed and solemn, looking like a bright-eyed fairy, perched at Mrs. Chichester's ear.

"Oh Flossie, how naughty!"

Florence shook back the fair hair from her face, and argued the matter.

"Flo is not naughty; Flo's good."

"I am afraid not, my darling;" and Dym finished her rebuke with a shower of kisses. "There, say good-night to Grannie."

"Florence has been saying such dreadful things," said Mrs. Chichester, gathering the child fondly in her weak arms; "she has been making poor grandmamma so unhappy. She tells me she wont love papa any longer."

"Oh Flo, for shame!"

"I think he is a naughty papa to stop away all this time," affirmed Flo confidently. "I don't think he is good, like grannie and mamma and auntie. I like auntie best," she whispered, as Dym carried her away. Dym, gravely kissing the little face before she left it, felt to-night as though the child's words had stricken her to the heart. Even Flossie was tired of waiting.

"I think I feel more restless than ever to-night," sighed Mrs. Chichester, as Dym sat down beside her. "Oh, that wind!"

"It is a rough lullaby certainly," returned Dym cheerfully, as she drew the heavy curtains closer, and looked to the fastening of the shutters, and then broke a blazing log into splinters. The white china tiles reflected the pleasant glow; the lamp burned brightly. Dym, as she read, stole a glance now and then at the white face lying on the pillow with blank open eyes, and thin hands fluttering aimlessly over the coverlet, and thought that, worn and faded as it had grown, it was beautiful still.

In spite of her efforts, Dym's voice would take tired tones now and then; her nerves were in a state of tension to-night; her reading was purely mechanical. Through it all she seemed to hear the dripping of the rain on the terrace as the wind lulled. Long before the usual hour Mrs. Chichester sent her away, pretending she could sleep; and Dym, with some reluctance, gave up her post to Dorothy.

It was her ordinary custom to go down and pat Kelpie and bid him good-night before she went to her own room, and however tired she was she never omitted the custom; but to-night Kelpie was not stretched as usual on the black bearskin in the library; he was whining restlessly at the foot of the stairs, as though he were weary of waiting for his young mistress.

Dym stooped down and caressed him; but though he licked her hand gratefully, he continued visibly uneasy, and trembled in every limb.

"Why, Kelpie, old fellow, what ails you? I suppose the wind is making you nervous too. One o'clock, and the storm shows no signs of lulling," as the glass in the conservatory rattled and shook in its frame, and the hail beat fiercely on the terrace outside. "What an awful night!" she thought, glancing round the dimly-lighted hall rather fearfully.

"Lie down, good dog," she said soothingly. But Kelpie resisted every effort to coax him to his bearskin; on the contrary, his restlessness increased; he whined, looked up in Dym's face, ran towards the door, and commenced sniffing under it, and then threw back his head with a low prolonged howl.

The dog's behaviour did not tend to reassure Dym; she knew the collie's sagacity was rarely at fault. For some reason or other he wanted her to open the door; perhaps some one was outside, most likely a tramp. Dym's imagination did not stretch to the idea of housebreakers, she had been too long an inhabitant of the happy valley for such a notion to enter her head; but still she was all alone. There might be two tramps perhaps, or even gipsies; she did not feel in the least disposed to open the door.

Again she attempted to coax Kelpie away; she even took hold of his collar, and tried to drag him with her two hands; but it was no use: the dog only growled at her reproachfully, and broke into a dismal howl. In another moment he would rouse the house.

"There can be no harm if I slip the chain and let him run through," she thought; "it is silly of me to be so frightened; perhaps, after all, it is only Sukey, or one of her pups, strayed up from the keeper's lodge." But for all that she was nervous, and bungled sadly over the bolts. She had miscalculated the distance. however—the dog, with all his efforts, could not squeeze himself through the aperture, and his bark of disappointment drove Dym's fears to the wind in the terror lest Mrs. Chichester should be alarmed. "Oh, hush, hush!" she cried, dropping the chain in desperation: she thought she could close the door quickly after him, but she had forgotten the wind. Kelpie had scarcely vanished into the darkness before a wild gust blew the door out of her hand, and drove her backward, pelting her face and dress with hailstones, and nearly lifting her off her feet.

All her strength could not have availed to close the heavy oak door; the servants slept far away, no one could hear her if she called; the lights were flaring, her hair and dress blew about wildly. All at once a low uncontrollable cry broke from her lips, and her knees trembled under her.

And why?

Because a warm human hand, groping in the darkness, suddenly touched hers; and a voice close by, speaking out of the storm and wind, said: "Don't be afraid. Kelpie knows me. I am Guy Chichester!"

## CHAPTER VII.

### LITTLE FLORENCE.

WHAT do we do in great crises of our life? How many of us can answer that question? Our friends know perhaps —as for us we are stricken dumb with a great silence.

Who is this breathing, living, moving being? Is it I? Do I feel all this? Is the clock striking? Am I awake? Is the world just as it was before this morning? By-and-bye we shall feel glad, or sorry perhaps; now we look on with blank eyes in which there is a little wonder, perhaps terror; presently we shall wake up we think and find it all a dream.

Dym never knew what she felt when that unlooked-for apparition crossed the threshold and drew her on with it, one faint cry she had uttered, half in recognition and half in terror, as that groping touch met hers in the darkness, but now she seemed stricken dumb.

Her limbs shook under her, and she leant against the wall to support herself as the strange bearded figure quietly closed the door and then stooped down to caress the dog that was shivering and whining about his feet. She could not have spoken, only when it turned and held out its hands to her in silence, the girl sprang forward and fastened on them, and her head was bowed lower and lower till it touched the rough coat sleeve.

He let her stand so for a minute as though speech was difficult even to him.

" Poor child, I never meant to frighten you in this way; it was Kelpie's fault, but it was brave of you to open the door."

" If I had only known—O Mr. Chichester !" Dym's voice had a quiver of ecstasy in it now.

" Somebody besides Kelpie has not forgotten me, I see," laying his hand on her hair. " Hush, my child, do not tremble so, it is no wraith, but a real flesh-and-blood Guy Chichester."

" Yes, I know—safe home. I said it—I felt it, thank God."

" Amen," returned Guy Chichester devoutly but the word was followed by a heavy sigh.

That sigh recalled Dym to herself.

The coming home might be joy to them—a bringing back from the dead—but what must it be to him? and then his mother.

" Come," she whispered, her soft cold fingers closing round his hand, and drawing him with gentle force ; " we must not stand here ; it would kill her if she heard your voice—with joy, I mean. They all thought you were dead—all but I—I never believed it. Come," and she led him to the dark library. Guy offered no resistance; he stood by silently, while Dym with shaking hands kindled the lamp she had always kept trimmed for his coming, and then set light to the piled-up logs. She did not rise from her knees till the dry wood spluttered and crackled into a blaze; even by the dim flare of the hall lamp she had seen he was dripping with wet from head to foot.

She stole a look at him now as she rose to her feet. He was no wraith, he had told her, and yet as he stood in his old position propping his broad shoulders against the mantelpiece it seemed to her that but for his voice she would hardly have recognised him. Was this their Sintram—the Guy Chichester they had missed for so many hopeless years—this tall haggard figure in sailor's dress? the brown bearded face looked thin and sallow and unkempt; there was a sunken weariness about his eyes, and his hair and beard were quite grey; he looked ten—twenty years older.

He turned and saw her watching him with her eyes full of tears.

"You don't know me, eh?" he said, with something of his old abruptness, only it was sharpened by pain. And as she came closer and put her hand timidly on his arm, as though she wanted the assurance of touch that this was really he, his closed over it quickly, almost eagerly. "Let me hold it a moment; I want to feel the touch of a woman's hand again. Good God, to think I have come to this! so they thought I was dead?"

"Humphrey said so, and Mr. Fortescue, and

I think your mother feared it at last. Mrs. Delaire put on mourning; they were all angry with me because I would not believe it."

"Humph," somewhat grimly, "I feel like a ghost revisiting my old haunts;" and then, as though the innocent pressure of the soft fingers soothed him, he said, half smiling, "then you did not believe it, eh?"

"I could not"—the tears brimming over her pale cheeks now. "I never had a doubt till this evening, when Humphrey fretted me. I knew— I was sure—you would come back to your child."

"Ah, heavens, my child!" the hollow eyes gathered a little light now, the hard muscles of the face relaxed, she had touched the right chord.

"She is such a darling, you will love her so," went on Dym hurriedly; "she has prayed every night for you ever since she could lisp your name."

"My little Florence," shading his eyes with his hand and speaking huskily now, "tell me more about them, Miss Elliott—my mother?"

"She is somewhat ailing," returned Dym evasively; but there was no eluding those stern sad eyes.

"I have a mother still, you are not trying to break any bad news to me? tut, how you frightened me, I saw a light in her window just now—she is ill then?"

"Very ill; I think the fear you were dead has broken her heart. She has been very weak, and they say she has no wish to rally; she will be better now, only——"

"Only what."

"She is blind."

"Again, good God!"

"You must not mind, it will be easier to bear now; it has all been so wretched. Hark, what is that?" as a crashing noise was heard outside. Mr. Chichester listened.

"One of the elms, I expect, has fallen into the carriage sweep. Ugh, what a night it is! all the storm fiends are abroad, I think."

"And you came home in spite of the storm?"

"Yes, I had got the home-sickness too strong to wait till the morning. A little extra buffeting would do me no harm, I thought; and then I saw the light in her window, and heard Kelpie bark. I knew when the door opened that I should see my little friend on the threshold."

"Kelpie found you — not I — good brave Kelpie."

"I was stealing away like a thief, when the rascal jumped on me; so I have friends still. Ah, well, I never dreamt of this—that I should be glad to come home even without her!"

"Are you glad, Mr. Chichester?"

"Yes, child, yes; I never thought to be thankful when He gave me back my life; but I am thankful now."

"Why?" she asked, speaking more to herself than to him.

"Why? have I not a child? I have been a poor father, perhaps, but it was the thought of her that kept the life in me, when one after another succumbed. I have looked death in the face more than once, but she has brought me back."

Dym shuddered; he was in the boat's crew after all; she had found the clue to his grey hair and hollow cheeks; he was gaunt through famine, worn by sickness, perhaps; the proud strength within him had given way under such cruel hardships.

" Why do you not take me to my child ?" he continued reproachfully; but Dym shook her head as she touched his wet sleeve meaningly.

" You must not go to her like this, you are wet through, Mr. Chichester. I will wake Stewart, and he shall bring you some dry clothes, and some wine."

" I would rather have some food," he returned shivering and holding his hands over the blaze; " I have learnt to bear hunger tolerably well," with a bitter smile, " but my endurance will not hold out much longer. Do you know I worked my way to Liverpool, and I had only money to pay my railway fare. I have not broken my fast since yesterday."

Dym uttered an exclamation of horror—he was starving and she had never offered him food; in what a pitiable plight had the master of Ingleside returned!

" Wait a moment," she gasped; she ran down the dark corridor that led to the servants' quarters. Stewart slept in a little room opening out of the butler's pantry; the lad stirred in his sleep as Dym shaded her lamp and called to him.

" It ain't time to get up, Miles, it is all that

old lying cock," he muttered drowsily. Dym had almost to shake him.

"Your master has come home—hush, don't wake the others; you must get up directly. I want wine, and food, and clothes for him; he is wet through and almost starving."

Stewart was wide awake after this; he found Miss Elliott loading a tray with food from the larder and took it from her without a word; his ruddy face was quite gaping and pale, as the gaunt, grey-haired figure in the ragged sailor's dress came eagerly forward.

"Is yon the master? I shouldn't have known him—we thought you was dead, sir," burst out poor Stewart, looking round-eyed and aghast. Guy held out his hand to him with one of his sad smiles.

"Miss Elliott took me for a ghost just now; don't be afraid, my good fellow, you don't know how sorrow and hunger change a man; when I have had something to eat and drink I may look more like myself."

Dym waited on him noiselessly—once as she was serving him with something, he took the little hand and carried it to his lips.

"If you knew what it is to me to have a woman's hand about me again," he said with some emotion. "I think your hair would rise, Miss Elliott, if you knew what I had been through," and for a long time after that he did not speak again.

Stewart came back by-and-bye with an armful of his master's clothes.

"I did it as quietly as I could," he whispered, "but Dorothy heard me and came to the door. I think the mistress is awake."

"I must go to her," returned Dym rising. "I was afraid of this. Wait with your master, Stewart."

Mrs. Chichester was sitting up in bed. She looked flushed and excited—her white hair had escaped from her cap, and lay in silvery lengths on her shoulder. Dorothy was smoothing it.

"Stewart has wakened my mistress," said Dorothy quickly. Dym tried to silence her with a look.

"What can Stewart be doing up here at this time of night, my dear? he was in Guy's room, I heard him. Dorothy would have it I was dreaming till she went herself to look." Dym stole an agitated glance at Dorothy, but the waiting woman's iron face was immovable as usual.

"I thought, maybe, he was walking in his sleep, only he had got some clothes over his arm; you haven't been to bed yourself, Miss Elliott, though it is nigh on an hour since you left us. Folks seem restless to-night," finished Dorothy, who had been disturbed from her own sleep, and was slightly impracticable.

"Is anything the matter? why have you not been to bed, my dear?" asked Mrs. Chichester anxiously. Dym was nearly at her wit's end. If Dr. Grey, or even Humphrey were here, to tell her what to do; she had heard that these sudden surprises were dangerous; and yet Stewart, and the clothes, and her own wakefulness—how was she to account for all that?

In desperation she went dangerously near the truth; Kelpie was restless. A poor man had taken refuge in their porch from the storm, and the dog had heard him; he was wet through and sadly in want of food, and she had wakened Stewart.

"A fine thing for Stewart to take his master's clothes," put in Dorothy, with a toss of her head; "poor man! most likely a tramp, or something worse; you oughtn't to have opened the door, Miss Elliott; it is not safe, he may be one of a gang, and the master's clothes, too."

"Dollie, whatever makes you so cross to-night? you are making Mrs. Chichester quite nervous with your fancies; he is only a poor homeless wanderer, and quite harmless," finished Dym, with a sudden choke.

"'He will come back, my girl.' Oh Will, dear Will, those brave words had come true."

"Maybe the mistress would be easier if I go down and have a look at him myself," returned Dorothy. Dym's agitation had not escaped her. Dorothy watched over her mistress's interest with a grim mastiff-like fidelity. Dym, in spite of her position at Ingleside, had often hard work to combat Dorothy's prejudices.

Dym gave herself up for lost as soon as Dorothy left the room, and then a sudden inspiration came to her.

"You don't think me wrong do you, dear?" she said, as she sat gently stroking the wrinkled hand, and trying to control the trembling of her voice. "Dorothy is very good, but she is hard sometimes; you would not have had me leave the poor man out in this dreadful storm."

"You might have sent him on to the lodge," replied Mrs. Chichester, doubtfully.

"You would not have said so if you had seen him. Mr. Chichester would have told me I was right, he never turned any one away."

A sort of spasm crossed the poor blind face; it was months since they had mentioned her son's name in her hearing.

"Oh, my boy! my boy! if I only knew where they had laid him!" she groaned; and then Dym knew that the hope had faded out of the mother's heart, and that she believed her son was dead.

If she should do harm instead of good. Dym was trembling so now that she could hardly speak.

"I want you to listen to me, dear. I have just heard such a strange story, it made me think of him and Will too. You will try to listen to me."

"I will try; but why did you mention his name? Oh, Guy! Guy!"

"This poor man, the one who is downstairs," went on Dym bravely, "left his home and all that was dear to him, because a great trouble had almost driven him mad, and he went away and wandered in foreign countries, and over great seas, just as your son has done."

"As Guy did, just as my boy did," and Mrs. Chichester rocked herself to and fro.

"He was so buffeted and tossed about that he hardly cared what became of him; he was shipwrecked, he suffered hunger and thirst, he saw his mates dying round him, and nothing kept his wretched life in him but the thought of his child."

"His child!" Mrs. Chichester's attention was arrested, she left off rocking herself to listen.

"He had only this dear little child to love him, except his mother, and he hardly knew whether he should find her alive—you are not listening to me, dear," cried Dym in a sort of agony, as her watchful ears caught the sound of approaching footsteps—they were advancing up the corridor, they came nearer and nearer—was Dorothy mad that she was bringing him to the very door?

"Not yet, oh, not yet!" she called out half beside herself and flinging her arms round the poor invalid, but the mother's ears were not to be cheated.

"You are hiding something from me—hark, what is that?" she exclaimed, pushing Dym away with weak arms that suddenly became rigid. "I tell you those are my boy's footsteps, it is Guy, he is not dead—my boy, my boy Guy!" but the shock was too great, the cry of joy died into a hoarse shriek, and as Guy sprang to her side she fainted away.

"Is she dead? Have I killed my mother?" Dym never forgot the white face of anguish with which Guy Chichester asked the question. Dym shook her head, as she applied the necessary remedies.

"Why did you not leave her to me? We were wrong all of us," she whispered presently. "I think you had better go away now, Mr. Chichester, it will be safer, much safer!"

"Don't send me away," he implored; "look here, Miss Elliott, she knows me," and the tears positively stood in Guy Chichester's eyes as the weak nerveless fingers closed round his hand. "You know me, mother, don't you?" he continued; "you know Guy has come back never to leave you again?"

Yes, she knows him now, as with her feeble strength she creeps closer to him and lays her poor blind face on his breast, "her son that was dead and is alive again;" they need not fear for her, such happiness seldom kills. Dym stands and watches them for a moment, and then steals softly from the room, beseeching Dorothy to follow her.

"What was that you said, Guy? tell it me again, my boy."

"I promised I would never leave you—you have a great deal to forgive, mother darling."

"No, you must never leave me again, my dear," passing her thin hand caressingly over the rough bearded face, "never again, my son. I think if you had stayed away a little longer, only a very little longer, Guy, my heart would have broken."

Flossie had such a queer dream that night.

She was fast asleep, oh, quite fast asleep she was sure, when a great bright round star as big as the moon went dancing round her bed and flared up in her eyes, and just as she called to Auntie to take it away, some one cried out quite loud, "Give me the light; I must see her, little Florence! little Florence!" and a tall man stooped over her and brushed her cheek with a long soft beard.

Flossie was quite sure too that after this Auntie cuddled her off to sleep, but Auntie was of another opinion, for as the child opened her dreamy eyes, Guy fell on his knees and called out her name with a sobbing spasm in his throat.

When Flossie fell asleep again it was in her father's arms, the golden head pillowed itself quite unconsciously on the rough coat, the dimpled arm flung itself with a child's carelessness across the broad heaving breast, and so through the long dark dawn, and far into the stormy March morning Guy Chichester kept watch and ward beside his child.

Flossie was slow in waking the next morning. A pleasant puzzle of thoughts came into her head; a cock was crowing somewhere; there was a great patter of raindrops against the windows; Flossie opened her eyes and began to count them. "One—two—three—four; what a many; I shall never do it; they are all having a game of play, and running after each other. Oh dear! oh dear!" yawned Flossie.

"That's right; open those pretty eyes, my

darling. Grey eyes! just like hers—just like hers."

Flossie was wide awake now, so why did she rub her eyes again and again? She was not dreaming, not a bit of it. There was the cock crowing, and there were the raindrops, and, close beside her, there was the same tall man she dreamt about last night.

Flossie was not a bit frightened, so she lay and looked at him—such an ugly man, with a great beard that hid his mouth, and rough grey hair, and great sad eyes that seemed familiar to her, perhaps—though he was so ugly — and then Flossie rubbed her eyes again.

"My little Florence, my own darling, do you know me?"

Florence nodded her head gravely, and pursed up her lips; evidently she was not prepossessed.

"Who am I? Speak, my pet."

"I suppose you are Papa," shrugging her shoulders, and then speaking confidently, "yes, I know you are Papa, though you are not a bit like your picture; and I don't believe"—patting her pillow rather crossly—"that I shall love you a bit."

"Oh Flo! Flo! how can you be so naughty?"

"Leave her to me, please, Miss Elliott," whispered Guy, but his brown cheek reddened a little; "so young a child is surely to be won. Answer me, sweet eyes, why do you think you will not love me?"

This puzzled Florence.

"If you are papa, you are not a good papa to stop away so long. Auntie and I have been quite tired of saying, 'God bless dear papa, for ever and ever, Amen!' for, oh! such a long time."

"Have you really prayed for me, my precious pet? Has Florence wanted her father?"

"Not much—at least auntie did. She used to cry nearly every day she talked about you. Do you love auntie, papa?"

"Very much," returned Guy gravely; but it must be owned that he hardly understood the question in the sudden thrill of ecstasy at hearing himself addressed for the first time by that title; it cost him an effort not to snatch the little creature to his breast and devour her with kisses, only he dreaded to alarm her.

Florence smiled, well pleased at his answer. She sidled up a little closer, stealing a small warm hand into Guy's shaking one.

"I think I shall like you after all, auntie does; and I love auntie best of all in the world."

"Oh, no; not best, Florence; you must surely keep the best for poor papa."

"Are you poor, papa? Aren't you happy? Do you want auntie and me to love you so very much, then?"

"I want you to love me, my little daughter—my heart's treasure—my only one;" and forgetful of his resolution, Guy held the fair little face between his hands and covered it with kisses; and then, as the child drew back startled at his vehemence, he took his seat quietly beside her, and, in an agitated voice, told her in the language best suited to her childish capacity, that he had been a long way— thousands and thousands of miles; that he had once been nearly drowned in the great dreadful sea; that he had been cold, and hungry, and thirsty; that he had loved her, and thought of his little daughter day and night, and had prayed to God to send him safe home to her. "And now I have come you must try to love me, Honor's dear baby, whom she left as her dying legacy; you will love me for poor mamma's sake, wont you, Florence?"

"She is—isn't poor mamma," returned the child indignantly; "mamma is a beautiful angel; auntie told me so. Were you very cold and hungry, papa? Are you warm now? Never mind, auntie and I will take such care of you."

"And you will love me, my pet?"

"Oh, yes; I don't mind your being ugly now, though your beard does hurt so. Put your head down on the pillow; I can reach you so; there, that is comfortable. One kiss for mamma— auntie told me to do it; and one for auntie; and three from little Florence. And why do you cry papa? I shall be a great girl soon, and then I shall be quite as good as mamma, you know."

Dym left the father and child together, and muffling herself up in her waterproof, and only taking the precaution to draw the hood over her

bright hair, ran down the terrace and across the
garden, and out of the little side gate leading to
the home-farm.

The first burst of mother's rapture; the child's
first recognition was over, and Dym's next
thought was for Humphrey; Humphrey must
know, and no one but she must tell him.

Running down the wet field-paths; battling
bravely with the wind and rain, and now and
then stopping to take breath, Dym sped light of
foot and light of heart till, turning the corner of
the farm buildings, she almost fell into the arms
of Humphrey himself.

"What's to do now—why, what in the name
of wonder brings you down to the farm, Dym?"
and Humphrey eyed the little hooded and cloaked
figure with growing perplexity and uneasiness.
"Madam isn't worse, is she?"

"She is better," returned Dym, breathlessly,
tossing back her hood, and displaying a very
rosy and happy face; "she is sleeping as sweetly
as a child, and as she has not slept for months;
and Dorothy is sitting beside her crying her eyes
out."

"Dorothy crying! You are in a crazy mood
this morning, Dym. Whatever brings you down
to the Five-acre on such a morning?"

"There is nothing the matter with the morning; I never thought rain so beautiful before.
I declare I hardly felt it; and I wanted so to
speak to you, Humphrey."

"I won't hear a word you have to say here,"
returned Humphrey, decisively; "if you are

clean daft, Dym, I must take care of you. Come under the eaves of the great barn, none of the men are about; and now tell me this wonderful piece of news."

"How do you know I have any to tell?" returned Dym with an attempt at her old pertness; "it is not the first time I have come over to the farm to talk to you."

"But it is the first time you have brought that sort of face with you," returned Humphrey shrewdly, and indeed Dym's dark eyes were bright with heart sunshine. "Shall I guess, Dym, or will you have the telling yourself?"

"You couldn't guess, Humphrey, if you were to try ever so. Stoop your head; I want to whisper; it is too good to say out loud. Who do you think is at Ingleside, Humphrey? O Humphrey, who do you think came home last night?"

Dym's whisper broke into a falter, but Humphrey, generally so slow of comprehension, heard it perfectly. He started, and then his eyes flashed.

"Not the Squire; oh, Dym, you can never mean that," and a strange shiver of repressed feeling ran through Humphrey Nethecote's frame.

"His very own self, but, oh such a wreck, Humphrey, grey-haired and thin, and years older. Will you rebuke me for my faith now, because I told his mother and child that he would surely come home again?"

"No, no, you were right, and I was wrong,

and thank God for it! The Squire has come home you say; nay, I am a trifle dizzy, Dym, tell it me over again. Why, we thought he was dead—Madam and all of us."

"Kelpie and I knew better—it was Kelpie who knew him first, and insisted on my unbarring the door. Come, Humphrey, you must not look pale over it; you are more startled because you lost all hope you see."

"Ay, ay, when I see him I shall understand it better. Come away, Dym, why are we waiting? The Squire will expect a welcome, of course."

Dym nodded assent, but she looked up anxiously into Humphrey's face as they threaded the wet field-paths again. Humphrey's face was quite blanched with his great surprise, and now and then he bit his lip nervously.

"The Squire's come home, and I thought he was lying fathoms deep," she heard him mutter to himself, and then, as though the real truth were suddenly dawning on him, he quickened his steps into a hasty stride.

"Gently, gently, Humphrey;" but for once he did not hear her. Dym's own footsteps became a run, and even then she only retained her place at his side with difficulty; she followed him panting as Humphrey pushed open the conservatory door, and advanced to the library; but there the old instinct made them both pause, and Dym timidly knocked.

"Who is there?—come in. What, Humphrey!" Guy put down his child from his knee and rose hastily, and the two men grasped hands in silence.

"Eh, Squire! but we have been heartsick for the loss of you, and the good God has given you back to us;" and Humphrey turned aside for a moment, and his face worked with emotion.

"I haven't deserved it, Humphrey," returned Guy in a broken voice, "any more than I deserve this welcome. I never thought that anything could be so sweet to me again. Look here, dear old friend, my more than brother!" and throwing his arm over Humphrey's broad shoulder he drew him to where the child sat watching them with solemn grey eyes of puzzled wonder.

"She is growing like Honor's self. I always said she would, Squire; she will be the light of your eyes and the sunshine of your home, before many years are over."

She has Honor's eyes and broad thoughtful brow; but she will never have her mother's beauty, and her hair is several shades lighter," added Guy, regretfully.

"Mamma is very pretty, but I think auntie is prettier," interrupted Florence. "Why do you look sad, papa? you are not hungry or cold now you know."

"No, not now, my darling," he replied fondly, snatching her again to his breast; "at least I can bear to endure my life now this one blessing is spared to me. I never thought to say that, Humphrey, till I knew how dreadful the shadow of the valley of death could be."

"Ay, we must all bide till our time comes," returned Humphrey, laconically; but as Florence nestled caressingly on her father's shoulder, the child's golden hair mingled with the Squire's grey beard, Dym saw him hastily turn away and brush his hand across his eyes.

## CHAPTER VIII.

### AT BAY.

THE news of the Squire's return spread like wildfire through the little valley of Birstwith, and before many hours were over Ingleside was besieged by friends and acquaintances of all degrees.

The vicar and his wife were the first arrivals, Mr. Fortescue as he entered the room and heard Guy's cheery, "Well, Lat, how has it fared with you, old fellow?" was so overpowered with emotion that he could only wring his cousin's hand without saying a word, while Katherine, silent and subdued for once in her life, kissed him affectionately and said, "God bless you, Guy!" and then indulged in a thorough womanly bit of crying.

"Who would have believed Kate had so much feeling in her," Mr. Chichester observed afterwards, but his own eyes glistened as he said it; through that day's ordeal the Squire bore himself bravely, but Dym noticed his face grew paler and graver, and his lips were often compressed as though in pain as he listened to his friends' kindly congratulations and warm expressions of joy.

Towards evening the terrace before the house was literally crowded with hosts of the farm-labourers anxious to catch a glimpse of the "Master, God bless him"—grey-haired patriarchs of the valley who had known him as a boy, some of the old almshouse men with a sprinkling of women and boys, and at the very edge of the group Gentle Florence in her grey duffle cloak, peering anxiously over Bob's shoulder. Guy singled her out at once with a greeting that made the little Quakeress crimson with pleasure; as one of his tenants and dependants he had a word and a hand-shake for every one of them; as he left them a ringing cheer startled the rooks into September cawing. "Three times three—that's right, my men; now you must drink the Squire's health one and all of you; you all know where the Squire keeps his home-brewed," and by this judicious hint Humphrey Nethersole rapidly cleared the terrace and grounds for the night. They could hear the cheers dying off merrily in the distance. Before long the valley was aflame with a red lurid light; a large bonfire was burning on the common. Humphrey called the Squire to look at it.

"Poor lads, it is their way of killing the fatted calf. I suppose we must give them a dinner or a supper; you must manage it, Humphrey," and then he sat down by his mother with a sigh and drew Florence to his knee, and for the rest of the evening he scarcely spoke, except in answer to their questions.

"Ay, but the Squire's sorely changed," was

Humphrey's parting observation that night; "he'll never be the man he was again," and before many days were over Dym coincided in Humphrey's opinion.

It was true that when the first excitement of coming home had a little subsided Guy became strangely taciturn and silent; he was very reticent on the subject of his wanderings, and evaded as far as possible all inquiries as to his escape from the burning vessel.

"Why should I speak of what causes me such acute suffering only in the retrospect?—you would not sleep to-night, mother, neither should I, if I were to recapitulate all the horrors of that ghastly scene," and Guy's shudder was sufficiently expressive.

"Let the dead past bury its dead," he said on another occasion, when Mr. Fortescue was questioning him; "don't let us rake up bygones, Lat, it was all a miserable failure from beginning to end—India or Australia, what did it matter? I took my trouble with me. I never got rid of it for a minute—and now."

"Well, Guy?"

"I have brought it back, that is all," and the dark moody look came across Guy Chichester's face as he put down his child from his knee and resumed his old restless walk across the room. But except when they questioned him about those dreary three years, he was ordinarily very gentle and quiet. It was beautiful to watch him with his mother and child. He would rouse himself from his melancholy brooding to sit by his mother's side and talk to her by the hour together, but it was evident that his one thought was Florence.

He was ill at ease if the child were out of his sight even for an hour; from morning to night he was devising little plans for her amusement. Florence's "new papa," as she called him, became her favourite playfellow. Guy's old spark of humour woke up when he told stories to his child. Often Humphrey would meet them on the farm, walking hand in hand, Guy's shoulders a little stooping, his head bent, Florence dancing beside him with her fair hair streaming in the wind

Guy bought a little cream-coloured pony and trained it himself; he taught Florence to ride, to her great delight. The Black Prophet was exercised regularly now. Dym, as she watched them from the terrace, was strangely reminded of the old days at Lansdowne House, when Edith and Cousin Guy used to ride out together.

Edith was growing up now, and was wintering at Mentone with her mother, who had become a confirmed invalid; but Beatrix Delaire had written that she might be expected at Ingleside in the course of a week or two.

Guy showed her letter to Dym.

"I hope you have forgotten your old antagonism," he said, with one of his old shrewd looks. "Poor Trichy! she has had her share of trouble with the rest of us."

"I think Mrs. Delaire has greatly improved since her residence abroad," returned Dym, magnanimously; "she is lovelier than ever, and has grown strangely gentle, even to me," laughing a little nervously.

"I am glad to hear it; I shall think better of her," was Guy's answer, and the subject dropped; but all that day and the next Dym took herself to task because the old uneasy feeling had returned at the thought that Mrs. Delaire was coming to Ingleside.

"It is so nice and quiet now, and when she comes she will monopolize him, and he will not find time to say a word to me," whispered jealousy. "He will always find time to remember his friends," added Dym's better monitor.

Dym was always taking herself to task now. Something unaccountable and wholly mysterious was troubling her sweet nature sorely. She was strangely happy and yet ill at ease, and never so ill at ease as in Guy Chichester's presence.

Dym told herself sometimes that she was growing jealous even of Florence. What if the father and child should become all in all to each other, and she were robbed of her darling? Dym cried shame on herself for this unworthy feeling; but she need not have feared—Florence was true to her old favourite, and often refused to accompany her father for a walk or drive unless Auntie were of the party.

"You see Florence has not learnt to do without me yet," Dym would say, a little sadly and apologetically when Mr. Chichester insisted on her accompanying them; "she will be wiser soon."

"When Florence learns to forget her old friends, she will be no daughter of mine," returned Guy, with one of his winning smiles. "Why will you consider yourself *de trop*, Miss Elliott? Do you think that no one besides Florence is pleased to have you?"

It was evident Guy Chichester had not forgotten his old favourite. There was a grave, almost a brotherly tenderness in his manner to her, that ought to have won her from her reserve now and then. He would bear himself towards her as though he felt himself her debtor. It was true the girl had endeared herself to him in no small degree by the filial care and love she had lavished on his mother.

"But for you she would not be alive to welcome me now, and the sin of having broken my mother's heart would have lain heavily at my door. You have saved me from this last bitterness, Miss Elliott; you have loved and guarded my motherless child for me, and yet you say I owe you no debt of gratitude."

"It was cancelled long ago, Mr. Chichester. I implore—I beg you not to say such things. Who was it who first befriended the lonely girl, and made her welcome in your own home? You have been my benefactor and friend ever since I first saw you," continued Dym in a voice of emotion, and then breaking down altogether.

"Have it your own way," he responded with a sad smile, holding out his hand; "you may close my lips, but you cannot prevent my feeling grateful to you with all my heart. Put me to the proof, Miss Elliott; see if there be anything that I would not do for your happiness if it were in my power." And there was a look in Guy Chichester's dark eyes as he said this that set the seal to his words.

Such speeches as these filled Dym's heart with a tumultuous happiness that was akin to pain. She would think over them with a beating heart, as she sat working silently by Mrs. Chichester's side.

She had grown very silent of late they told her. Dym used to smile at the accusation, but all the time she knew it was true. When Mr. Chichester was in the room she felt strangely tongue-tied—a new sort of shyness oppressed her; she had an odd trick of flushing up when he looked at or spoke to her. Dym could not understand what ailed her; she had lost all her old fearless ways, and yet she only told herself that it is because this long absence had made her friend strange to her.

"I have something against you, Miss Elliott," Guy said to her one day, when they were alone together in the drawing-room—it was the evening that Mrs. Delaire was expected, and the carriage had been sent down to the station. Dym, who had made her toilette early, was kneeling on the rug in the firelight, caressing Kelpie, when Mr. Chichester came in.

Dym rose with a sudden blush, and seated herself in silence.

"Against me, Mr. Chichester!"

"Ay," he returned, with a penetrating glance, as he took his old attitude against the mantelpiece. "I have long wished to ask you something. I want to know what has become of my little friend?"

"I don't understand you!" stammered Dym; but she grew rosy notwithstanding.

"I saw her last on the threshold of the door one wild March morning, when Kelpie scented his master. She was sufficiently benevolent to throw the door wide open for him to enter, but"—with a singular emphasis—"I have never seen her since."

Dym coloured high; she was beginning to grasp his meaning.

"What has become of her, Miss Elliott, I should like to know? She had her faults, but want of affection and candour was not among them. Do you know I miss my little friend every day?"

"She is here!" in a voice barely above a whisper.

Mr. Chichester smiled.

"I don't think so. Miss Elliott, have you grown to be afraid of me?"

"Not very." Dym was crimson now.

"A little, then!"

"I don't know; anyhow, I cannot help it, Mr. Chichester."

He shook his head indulgently.

"Out of sight is out of mind. Fie! Miss Elliott, I would not have believed it of you."

"Oh, no; it is not that," she exclaimed

eagerly, roused at last into defending herself, but stammering still; "I have not forgotten you, Mr. Chichester—how could I? only it is all so strange, and you are altered, and——."

"I am not altered to you"—somewhat pointedly—" and as for the outward man——" he sighed; and then went on in the same gentle tone, "Child, I don't like to see you shy and shrinking from me somehow; it hurts me. Though my hair is grey, and my heart well nigh broken, I have still some old affections for my friends; and I ever held you as one of them."

"Oh! Mr. Chichester!" But Dym had no time to say any more; for at that moment the carriage-wheels sounded in the entry, and Mr. Chichester hastened out to welcome his cousin.

Dym was not present at their meeting; but she noticed that Beatrix looked pale and agitated when she came into the room a few minutes later leaning on her cousin's arm. She greeted Dym with so much kindness that Guy had reason to conclude the old antagonism was dead and buried; and even Dym, who always in her secret heart accused Beatrix of artifice in her simplest words and actions, was not proof against the gentleness that disarmed her.

No one could believe Beatrix was acting a part who saw her that evening. Generally cold and undemonstrative, she was affectionate in her demeanour to her aunt, lavish of caresses to little Florence, while her joy at seeing her cousin again was evidently deep and earnest.

If Beatrix had set herself to charm them all she could not have succeeded better. Guy, who was generally silent and restless after Florence had gone to bed, now joined the fireside group, and seemed interested in the description of a trip to the Pyrenees that Beatrix was giving her aunt, and now and then he could not help owning to himself that Miss Elliott was right in declaring that his cousin was lovelier than ever.

Beatrix's face and form had always seemed to his fastidious taste well-nigh faultless, though it had been somewhat marred by a repellent haughtiness and a cold searching look in the eyes; this was exchanged now for a softened bearing, and the transparent complexion was now perfectly dazzling in contrast to her deep mourning dress.

"I believe my poor Undine has found her soul after all," was Guy's secret comment, "perhaps after all she liked Frank more than we thought. And with his old kindliness Guy Chichester set himself to make his cousin's visit pleasant to her.

It was the old mistaken kindness, but it failed to achieve its object.

For some days, more than a week indeed, everything went on smoothly at Ingleside. Beatrix's white brow wore a peaceful unruffled look that had long been a stranger to it; she made herself quite at home in Mrs. Chichester's boudoir and in the Squire's study, she helped her cousin with his accounts, rode out with him and Florence, and already village gossip reported that the beautiful widow would eventually take up her residence at Ingleside. "Ay, she is a rare beauty, but she is not so real bonnie as t'ither were," as one of the old women at the almshouses was heard to say; "she hasn't a glint of sunshine in her face, there's no one like 'the good lady.'"

Guy smiled scornfully when these reports reached him.

"Slanderous fools!" he muttered. "Do they think I would replace Honor? Poor Trichy, I hope this will not reach her ears—it would annoy her dreadfully."

But it was not village gossip that brought the first cloud on Beatrix Delaire's face—a trifle, a word had revived the old soreness. One day Dym felt there was an imperceptible change in Beatrix's manner, and taxed all her efforts to discover the cause, but in vain.

"I have not slighted her in any way," thought Dym, "it must be my fancy." But the next day it was there, and the next also.

Could it be that Beatrix resented Dym's position at Ingleside, that she was jealous of Florence's devotion, of her aunt's warm love for her adopted daughter, that Guy's friendship was displeasing to her? "She never liked me to have much to do with him," thought poor Dym.

Dym was half right and half wrong in her surmise as to Mrs. Delaire's changed manner; Beatrix had made up her mind to accept Dym as a necessary evil, and to tolerate her position at Ingleside with as good a grace as possible—

come what might she would not quarrel with her. Guy had his whims and this was one of them, and she did not choose to incense him against her.

Beatrix was determined to be perfectly good-humoured and to patronize Miss Elliott. She personally disliked her—Beatrix always disliked those she had injured—but her repugnance had to be conquered or hidden.

"It is love me, love my dog," she thought, smiling bitterly at her cousin's autocratic ways; "it is a pity he is so foolishly Quixotic. I wonder if he will ever care for a woman after Honor?" and Beatrix sighed as she thought of the strong tenacity of Guy Chichester's affection. For a time Beatrix found her rôle perfectly easy, and then all at once her manner changed.

And why?

Because the widow's shrewd cold eyes had read Dym's innocent secret—the secret unguessed even by herself—and she had determined that at all hazards Dym must be removed from Ingleside.

"If he finds it out, as he surely will, he will only pity her, and—well, one never knows to what length men like Guy can go; he must never know it, never. If I ventured to warn her in a friendly way," and Beatrix rose from her low seat, and began pacing the room with troubled steps.

"I think I shall venture it. She will fly into a passion in her old way, and call me her enemy. Are we enemies, I wonder? What made me dislike this girl from the first? If I were superstitious I should say she crossed my path in **an** evil day. Honor Nethecote was not specially dear to me, but one was obliged to respect her in spite of one's hatred, but Miss Elliott——" Here Beatrix's uneasy cogitations were interrupted by the entrance of Miss Elliott herself.

Dym came into the room smiling. "Mr. Chichester wants to know if you will ride with him. Florence and he are going over to Ripley; it is such a beautiful day, and—are you not well, Mrs. Delaire?" Dym had certainly some reason in asking the question. Beatrix looked pale and worn; at such times her face would look almost old.

"Yes—no—I am not very well this morning. Tell my cousin, please, Miss Elliott, that I will not ride; give him my love; say I have a fit of the vapours—anything you like."

"If you are dull, shall I come and sit with you?" asked Dym, timidly. Somehow the young figure in its deep mourning always evoked her sympathy; instinctively she felt that Beatrix Delaire was unhappy, and the generous girl longed to comfort her.

"Yes, if you like," answered Beatrix, indifferently, but under her cold demeanour her heart was throbbing loudly. Was this her opportunity? Should she speak to her now? She must dissemble, and pretend kindness, she thought to herself. In spite of her habitual insincerity, Beatrix felt this thing was not easy to be done.

Dym found her sitting by the fire in deep thought, with her head resting on her hand. As

Dym took the seat beside her she suddenly shivered and moved slightly.

"I am sorry to see you so ill, Mrs. Delaire."

Beatrix smiled bitterly.

"I am never ill; have you ever heard me complain, Miss Elliott?"

"You are unhappy, then?" in Dym's softest tones.

"Well, perhaps you are right; something has occurred to trouble me, that is all."

"I am sorry," began Dym, but Beatrix interrupted her almost fiercely.

"I suppose you would be surprised if I told you that you yourself were the cause of my trouble, Miss Elliott."

"Who, I—I hope—that is, I trust I have done nothing to offend you?" stammered Dym.

There was a strange earnestness and abruptness in Beatrix's manner that startled her, but the next moment it had wholly changed.

"Offended me, my dear Miss Elliott? No, you have only made me think," in a soft, melancholy voice. "I cannot help being very sorry for you, that is all.",

"Sorry for me!" Dym's cheeks were flaming now.

"Yes; you are so singularly placed, and my aunt is so injudicious—so helpless, I mean. If I were not afraid of making you angry, I think I should try and warn you of something, but I dare not provoke the hasty temper I remember so well, Miss Elliott."

Dym lifted her hot face bravely.

"I hope I have learned to control it now. You frighten me, Mrs. Delaire. What have I done to pain you?"

"Nothing," replied Beatrix, laying her hand lightly on hers for a moment. Somehow Dym quite shuddered away from the cool polished touch. "Why will you persist in thinking that you have offended me, if I am only speaking as your friend?"

"My friend!" Dym could not suppress that exclamation. A flush crossed Mrs. Delaire's face as she heard it.

"You distrust me still," she said, drawing herself up proudly; "you have never forgotten the old grudge when we were girls together, Miss Elliott. If you will not believe I mean it for your good, at least you know me to be interested in my cousin's welfare?"

"Why do you bring in Mr. Chichester's name?" asked Dym, in a bewildered voice.

"Because what I have to say concerns him closely, Miss Elliott. You will hate me outright I know; but I must speak. I must warn you that your continued residence under my cousin's roof is perilous to your peace of mind. Don't misunderstand me," she continued, eagerly; "no one has told me—I have found it out myself. Probably you are not conscious of it yourself; but it is as true as the heavens above us, that you are not indifferent to——" She stopped. "Miss Elliott, do you dare affirm that you do not love my cousin Guy?"

At this unexpected and cruel thrust Dym

grew as white as death, and her head dropped on her bosom; for a moment she shrunk back as though she had received a visible blow.

Beatrix took her unresisting hand gently.

"You need not answer—I can see it for myself. I have always been afraid of this—always. Others have been to blame, not you; you ought not to have been placed in such a position."

The poor white face before her, stricken with sudden shame and dismay, moved even her to pity.

"You must not take it like this, Miss Elliott; who could be long with Guy without loving him?" and Beatrix sighed. "These sort of feelings come gradually; you were not aware of them yourself."

"I did not know. Oh, this is too dreadful!" suddenly exclaimed Dym. Her innocent appealing eyes smote Beatrix's cold selfishness with tardy remorse; the absolute purity of her look almost inspired her with awe.

"If this were true, and I knew it," went on Dim with a trembling lip; "you would do well to scorn me. I should not be worthy the name of woman; but I never—never—thought it was that." And a sudden overpowering blush finished her sentence.

"I can well believe it," began Beatrix, soothingly; but Dym put out a shaking hand and stopped her.

"Please don't speak to me; you mean it kindly, but I cannot bear it. I was going to say perhaps I ought to have known it; but he was so far above me I thought there was no danger; and I had no mother, not even Will to warn me."

She covered her face and wept passionately; steadfast in her young truth it never came into her mind to defend herself, to disarm suspicion by a pretence of well-merited anger. "Dare you affirm that you do not love my cousin?" Beatrix had said to her; and the words had brought their own conviction.

Yes, she loved him; she knew it now, innocently as a child, purely as a girl, blindly as a woman. Out of that singular friendship had come the anguish of a hopeless first love; she had dared to love her benefactor. Dym was cowering away from the thought like a frightened dove, only one idea was in her mind. Mrs. Delaire was right, and she must leave Ingleside.

No one need have envied Beatrix's feelings as she sat silently beside the weeping girl. Her victory humiliated and punished her; in all her life she had never acted so base a part. Miss Elliott had never injured her, yet she was going near to break her heart; she was disturbing the domestic circle she had come to visit; through her means, her aunt, helpless in her blindness, would lose her adopted daughter, Florence her loving nurse and friend. Beatrix did not wrong the nobility of Dym's nature; she knew she would leave Ingleside; but some word she did say as to her own want of generosity.

"Perhaps I ought not to have said this. Will it make us enemies again, Miss Elliott?"

"You meant it for the best. I suppose one ought not to be allowed to walk beside a precipice unwarned; but I think I could have borne it better from any one else."

"You have always distrusted me," returned Beatrix, icily; "but at least you know I have my cousin's interests at heart."

"I shall not wrong them," was the sad answer. "You need not fear that I shall stay here, Mrs. Delaire; nothing could keep me here now— nothing—nothing!" clasping her hands in despair in spite of herself.

Mrs. Delaire could not help admiring the girl's courage and resolution.

She watched her for a moment, almost enviously; the slight girlish figure, the drooping head, the little dark face that had suddenly grown so wan and wistful.

"I suppose I may go now?" Dym said, turning to the door.

She did not wait for any answer; she almost staggered when a rush of April sunshine met her outside, the sweet spring sunshine that pervaded everything. Downstairs in the hall, doors were opening and shutting; Florence's baby laughter sounded from the terrace, Guy's grave voice answering. "Run in, my darling; these northern winds are treacherous," she heard him say.

Dym leant against the wall, faint and dizzy. Was she never to hear that voice again? was he to miss his little friend every day—always? was she to go away from them all?

"Oh, Will! Will! if I could only die!" groaned the unhappy girl, hiding her face in her hands, and a horror and darkness of despair fell upon her.

## CHAPTER IX.

#### DARKEST BEFORE DAWN.

EVERYONE thought that Miss Elliott looked strangely ill that night.
The Fortescues and Trevors and Humphrey Nethecote were dining up at the Great House that evening, and Dym, who had spent the afternoon in her own room in a confused trance of suffering, had been obliged to rouse herself at last, and after bathing her aching eyes and head, to creep downstairs, trusting that under the shade of the friendly twilight she would be able to steal to her usual corner beside Mrs. Chichester without challenging special observation. But on this occasion the Fates were against her.

The lamps were already lighted as she entered the drawing-room. Humphrey had possession of her corner, and the Squire, contrary to his usual custom before dinner, was lounging on the rug in his favourite attitude, carrying on a somewhat one-sided conversation with his cousin.

Beatrix was not quite so ready as usual with her answer; she appeared absent and ill at ease. She started almost nervously as Dym entered;

a quick flush passed over her face—Guy did not seem to notice it—he talked on indolently till Humphrey's shocked voice reduced him to momentary silence.

"Why, Dym, whatever have you done with yourself? Some one told me you were ill," he began, in his cheery good-natured way.

"I have had a bad headache," stammered Dym, taking refuge in a seat beside Mrs. Chichester, and wishing in a sort of agony that Humphrey would desist from his questions; she commanded her voice with difficulty, so as not to alarm Mrs. Chichester, who was always anxious when anything ailed her favourite.

"You must have a shocking headache, my dear, for your hands are like ice, and your face was quite burning when you kissed me just now."

"The fire is so hot," returned Dym, struggling for composure, and shielding her face with her hand. "Humphrey, would you mind handing me that screen? Thank you. I am only a little faint—I shall be able to talk presently," and she gave him such an appealing glance to be silent, that Humphrey, sorely perplexed as he was, could nor fail to comprehend her, and at last consented to leave her in peace.

Dym drew a long breath of relief as he left her. Her screen shielded her from observation; Mr. Chichester was still talking, he had not noticed her then; if she could only elude his penetrating eyes all would be well; she must get through this evening, by-and-bye there would be time to think and to form her plans.

"Do you think you need come in to dinner, Miss Elliott?" Dym started, and the screen fell from her hand; Mr. Chichester quietly restored it. He had come noiselessly round to her side and was leaning on his mother's chair, but his question was so low-toned that it only reached the ear for which it was intended.

"Thank you, I have only a bad headache, it will go off presently," faltered poor Dym. She did not dare lift her eyelids, but the grave comprehending tenderness of Mr. Chichester's voice brought the colour to her face.

"Is there any necessity to put such a force on yourself?" he persisted gently; "you are either very ill or very unhappy. I wish"—in a half-whimsical, half-serious tone—"I wish I knew what was troubling my little friend."

"Don't, Mr. Chichester; oh, if you would only leave me," gasped out the poor child; she really hardly knew what she was saying, her temples throbbed with nervous agony, a dull sickening pain was at her heart, she felt physically faint and ill. "If only he would not be kind to her," she said to herself. "If she could only go away somewhere out of the reach of his voice." She had a dull sort of consciousness that she had been taken at her word, that Mr. Chichester was gone and his place was taken by Humphrey.

"You are not to come down to dinner, the Squire forbids it," he whispered loudly. "Perhaps the quiet may do your head more good. "I heard him order Stewart to bring you some strong coffee; try and rest a little; and perhaps in an hour you may be better." Dym gave a feeble smile in answer. When the room was empty, she took possession of one of the couches and drank her coffee; how good of him to interpose and shield her in this way; how could she have sat through the long dinner between Mrs. Trevor and Humphrey, and opposite Beatrix's scrutinizing eyes? "Perhaps he only thinks I am ill, and will forgive my petulance; but how could I tell him to go away when he was so kind —so very kind?"

Dym was able to pronounce herself somewhat better when the ladies made their appearance in the drawing-room. She shrank away from Mrs. Delaire's advances, however, and placed herself under Mrs. Trevor's wing.

Mr. Chichester found them talking, to all appearance very comfortably.

"Has my prescription taken effect?" he said, standing opposite them, and giving Dym one of his most critical glances. Dym felt his tone was a little cool.

"My head is certainly less troublesome," she returned, evasively. "The coffee was much better than the dinner, Mr. Chichester."

"Humph," was his sole answer, turning on his heel, and for the rest of the evening he did not again approach her corner.

Dym slipped away as soon as the guests had gone. She made some hasty excuse that Mrs. Chichester wanted her, and did not again re-enter the drawing-room, where Guy and his cousin were the only occupants.

12—2

Florence was awake for a wonder. Dym lay down on the bed beside her, in her white dress, and took the little creature in her arms, and waited patiently till she had fallen asleep with her head on her shoulder. "She would not hold her often in this way," she thought; and all at once it came into her mind how sadly Flossie would miss her. "She loves her father dearly, but she has not given him all her heart," she said to herself. And involuntarily she pressed the sleeping child closer to her breast as the prospect of their speedy separation came upon her. Dym never knew how the long hours of that night passed away; she could hear the church clock chiming out the quarters one by one. Presently the cock crowed, and a faint dusky light came stealing up the valley, her eyeballs burnt, the dull heavy throbbing at her head went on ceaselessly; towards morning fatigue and pain overpowered her, and she slept. Phyllis found her later on still in her white dress with Florence nestled close beside her.

"Why, you have never been to bed at all, miss," gasped out Phyllis, open-eyed and anxious; "dear heart, you will take cold and be sick, and no wonder, neither."

"Hush Phyllis! I fell asleep without undressing, that was all; it was very wrong, please say nothing of this to Dorothy." Dym felt she had been incautious when she saw Phyllis's puzzled look of alarm. She dressed quickly, and was in her accustomed place at the breakfast table long before Mrs. Delaire made her appearance. Guy and his child came in later hand-in-hand.

"I hope you are better this morning, Miss Elliott," Beatrix had said to her. Mr. Chichester merely gave her a scrutinizing glance as he shook hands.

"What are you going to do with yourself this morning, Trichy?" he observed as he sat down.

"I thought, perhaps, as it is so fine we might ride over to Knaresborough," she returned; "it is too far for Florence, but you and I might go."

He shook his head.

"You must leave me out, if you please. I have business this morning."

"Not those tiresome farm accounts, Guy? they could wait, surely; and these April mornings are so delicious." There was a trace of impatience in Beatrix's tone.

"I will send down a note to Latimer; it is a pity you should be disappointed of your ride," returned her cousin quietly. "My business is almost as unfortunate as your fit of the vapours yesterday, eh, Trichy?" and there was a lurking tone in Guy's voice that made Beatrix colour with vexation. Do what she would, she could not make this man yield to one of her caprices; he would set aside her requests in the coolest way if they did not meet with his approval.

She rose from the table now with a displeased air.

"Do not trouble yourself to send a note to the Vicarage. You know I dislike Mr.

Fortescue's company—if you will not ride with me yourself, Guy, I do not wish for any other escort."

"To-morrow, then," he returned good-humouredly; "suppose you keep my mother company this morning;" and Beatrix, vexed as she was, did not dare to press the matter closely.

Dym had left the room, and was hurrying across the hall when she heard Mr. Chichester's step behind her.

"Miss Elliott, have you any very pressing duty summoning you at the present moment?"

"I was going up to Mrs. Chichester—she expects—that is—I always read to her in the morning."

"Headache or no headache, I suppose? I have sent my cousin Beatrix to sit with her—come in here a moment, please, I want to speak to you;" and Mr. Chichester opened the library door. But Dym for the first time in her life hesitated to obey.

"I must go; I am sure your mother wants me," she persisted, keeping her ground. But her colour varied dangerously.

Mr. Chichester gave her one of his peremptory looks.

"Do you wish me to remind you that I have a right to be obeyed," he said, so gravely that Dym did not venture on a second remonstrance. Mr. Chichester's slight austerity vanished as he placed a chair for her.

"You are so unlike yourself that you make

me unlike myself," he said, with a smile that was evidently meant to atone for his speech: "come, Miss Elliott, drop this reserve that so ill becomes you, and tell me frankly what ailed you last night."

The question was so sudden and so unexpected, that Dym lost her presence of mind. "Don't ask me. Oh, I'm so unhappy!" she said hiding her face in her hands.

"So I suspected," was the quiet answer; "you are not subject to fits of vapours, too, are you? Come," and the shielding hands were taken down and held for a moment, "don't treat me to women's most persuasive arguments, you know what a horror men have of tears, but tell me—I have a right to know—what has been troubling you."

His voice with its old, kind drollery touched on too painful a chord. Dym snatched her hands away, and for a little while answer was impossible. Only between the slender girlish fingers the hot tears fell fast—tears of sorrow and shame—of doubt and bitter yearning.

Mr. Chichester stood looking at her for a moment, and there was a shade on his face as he turned away and walked slowly up and down the room; evidently there was something here for which he was not prepared. He had had one glimpse of her face before she had hidden it from his view, and its wild look of sorrow almost appalled him.

Dym hoped he would leave her; but he was only giving her time to recover herself.

Presently, when she had grown a little calmer, he took the seat beside her.

"Miss Elliott, do you know you are trying my patience sorely? No; no more tears, my child"—with a touch of peremptoriness. "I see I shall have to make you afraid of me after all. What has my cousin said or done to annoy you?"

No answer—only the tell-tale crimson mounting to the very roots of her hair.

"Beatrix and you had a long talk together yesterday. Trichy had a fit of vapours, which certainly lasted all the evening, for I never saw her so unlike herself; even Mrs. Fortescue noticed it. And I have never known you before suffer from these intense sick-headaches."

"One must be ill sometimes," she returned evasively.

"Do you think it cures them to do without your night's rest; you understand nursing very poorly"—with a keen glance that made her shiver. How had her long vigil reached his ears; could Phyllis have betrayed her?

Her miserable night was not the best preparation for the endurance of the day's trial. Dym felt so weak and wretched that she was utterly defenceless; not a spark of her old courage remained. She must guard her secret; so much her woman's pride told her; but after that it mattered little what became of her.

The pale rigidity of her features smote Guy Chichester's heart with generous pity.

"Forgive me if I pain you," he continued, gently, "but it is my duty to find out this.

Would you rather have me speak to my cousin?"

"No—oh no!"—in a deep voice of misery.

"Then you must be perfectly frank with me yourself. Tell me, Miss Elliott, have Beatrix and you quarrelled?"

Dym considered a moment. "Not in the way you mean—we disagree in opinion, that is all. Wait a moment"—pressing her hands on her temples in a bewildered sort of way, as though trying to collect her thoughts for a great effort—"I want to tell you something, Mr. Chichester, you may have to know it soon—I have made up my mind to leave Ingleside."

"To leave us!"—in a tone of astonished incredulity.

Dym had made a desperate plunge; she went on rapidly. "It was you who brought me here first, and you have a right to know. Flossie can do without me now, and your mother will easily find some one else to replace me. I have quite made up my mind to go; nothing you say can shake my resolution."

"Then in that case I need not try," was the somewhat dry rejoinder. "I suppose I may ask the reasons for this sudden and singular resolution?"

Her reasons! Dym was reduced to silence now.

"Have I unfortunately done anything to displease you?"

"You, Mr. Chichester!—oh no." Dym's grateful look was sufficiently eloquent.

"My mother, then?"

"Your mother is goodness itself. She is the dearest, the kindest——" Dym was nearly breaking down again.

"Then it is as I suspected, and Beatrix is at the bottom of the mischief. Oh, you women!" getting up from his seat and pacing the room impatiently. He was becoming angry now.

"Mrs. Delaire has never liked my being here," went on Dym in a stifled voice; "she says and thinks things that make me wretched."

"Has she said anything that makes it impossible for you to remain?" demanded Mr. Chichester, sternly. There was no misunderstanding his meaning: Dym grew whiter and whiter under those searching eyes.

"You need not answer. I begin to have a glimmering of the truth now. You could not tell me this yourself, of course. Never mind, I will take steps to silence Beatrix's nonsense. I would not have believed it of her," he muttered, still more angrily.

He was about to leave the room, when a sudden thought seemed to strike him, and he made a hasty stride back to her chair.

"If I make it all right—if Beatrix apologizes—you will not persist in your foolish intention of leaving us?"

She shook her head sorrowfully. "There is no apology needed. You are mistaken, Mr. Chichester. I must go."

"Nonsense," he continued impatiently; "you know so little of the world that you are not competent to decide on this point. Fools will talk; but wise men will not heed them. You are justly hurt and aggrieved; when you are older these things will not sting quite so badly. Leave me to bring Beatrix to reason; she shall apologize to you before many hours are over. Don't you know it would break my mother's heart to lose her adopted daughter?" He was turning away again, but Dym sprang after him and laid her hand on his arm: her face was perfectly ghastly.

"Mr. Chichester, you must not; I cannot bear it."

"I must not do what, my child?"

"Speak to your cousin. She is not to blame; she meant to be most kind. It is not her fault that I am in a false position; it is my own wish. I must go."

His pertinacity seemed cruel. It was depriving her of her last chance.

"You must allow me to judge whether I am to speak to my cousin or not," and there was a touch of haughtiness in Mr. Chichester's manner. Dym's look of mingled reproach and despair protested silently against his harshness.

"Can you not trust me?" he asked more gently. "Your brother would not have recommended your acting for yourself in such an emergency."

"O Will! Will!" Dym could not quite suppress the ring of misery in her voice. She let Mr. Chichester place her passively in a corner of the couch. Even before he left the room her head dropped on the cushions with a child's utter abandonment of weakness. She had fought out her piteous little battle, and had been worsted. In spite of her desperate determination, she had felt a very reed in the hands of this man, whose will was so strong and arbitrary for good. He had not suspected her secret, he had attributed her reluctance to remain to mere motives of maidenly modesty. Beatrix had told her she was in a false position, but would Mrs. Delaire guard it equally well? Dym in her innocence thought she would certainly try to shield her, and if it had not been for Beatrix's evil temper she would have been perfectly right in her surmise.

But Guy knew how to be provoking, and it was not easy to evade his lynx-like vigilance. The interview between the cousins was a long and stormy one, and when it was over Beatrix shut herself up in her own room for the remainder of the evening.

When a short time had elapsed, Dym made an attempt to go up to Mrs. Chichester, but the first movement brought back dizziness and faintness, and she was obliged to remain in enforced idleness. Phyllis brought her luncheon. Mrs. Chichester had gone down to the Vicarage, Mrs. Fortescue had sent for her and Florence. Phyllis thought Mrs. Delaire had gone with them. The Squire had started for a long walk with Kelpie, and Mr. Nethecote had sent up to know how Miss Elliott was.

"And I might have told him, miss, you were looking rarely worse, for there isn't a speck of colour in your face," added Phyllis in a vexed voice. Dym smiled faintly. It was a relief to own herself really ill, and decline the tempting meal Phyllis's foresight had prepared. She drank some wine and lay down again. This perfect quiet was bracing her numb faculties to fresh efforts. She must face her difficulties, and not sink under them; she thought, come what might, she must not forfeit her own self-respect.

She had fallen into a slight doze in the twilight, and had just wakened with a start, when there was a light tap at the door, and Mr. Chichester entered.

"You are just where I left you this morning," was his only greeting. "I told them not to disturb you. I hope you have properly repaired last night's ravages."

"I am better, very much better," she answered gratefully; "has Mrs. Chichester returned yet?"

"Yes, my mother has come back, I believe. I saw Florence just now," rather absently. "Miss Elliott, without renewing our previous conversation, I want you to make me one promise."

"If I can—that is, if it be right," she returned timidly, glancing up at him. Was it the firelight, or did his face look strangely pale and drawn.

"Promise me that you will not speak to my mother about leaving us for three days, not till I have spoken to you again—only three days remember."

"I can easily promise that."

"Beatrix tells me she had no intention of hurting you with ill-timed advice—we must give people their due—we all have our faults. If I might venture on giving you advice, Miss Elliott, it would be to dismiss all this from your mind for the next three days; be calm, be content, and trust me." As he spoke he put his hand upon her head with a fatherly gesture; and looking up, she saw the sad kindly gleam of his eyes.

A moment after the door closed, and Guy Chichester was alone—never more alone!

Alone! Alas, what bitter thoughts were lining the man's brow as he stood with arms tightly folded across his breast, and the flickering firelight playing on his bowed head and grey beard.

"Who would have thought of this," he muttered. "Poor innocent child, and to think Beatrix is making her her dupe; there was heartbreak in her face. I could see it for myself, and yet fool that I was never to dream of that; and then my mother and Florence—Florence will fret herself to death for her. Is there no other way, no other way but this? O Honor my darling, my darling, the only woman I ever loved, or that I ever can love, come to me one moment and tell me what I am to do in this sore strait." He spread his hands with a groan into the empty air, and then they dropped heavily to his side. Alas, these hours of desolation and anguish were not new to the lonely man, but to-night his soul was torn by conflicting passions, generous pity for the girl he had befriended; tender compassion for his mother and child, whose lives were so closely bound up with hers. At times the whole chivalry of his nature seemed to rise up and plead for these defenceless ones. " If I can make them happy, what does it matter what becomes of me ?" he thought. " She will be a mother to my child; she has never known any other; she is the sunshine of our house. Lonely as I am now, I feel I shall be doubly so if she leave us—no, for my own sake I cannot let her go; and yet is there no other way than this ?" He sighed heavily as the gong disturbed him from his musing. It was a silent party that gathered round the dinner-table that night; Beatrix was absent, the Squire taciturn and gloomy, Dym sad and conscious, and shrinking from notice. Once, and once only during the evening Guy roused from his reverie. Florence had clambered up into Miss Elliott's lap for a good-night kiss. Mr. Chichester suddenly raised his eyes and regarded the pair long and fixedly. The child had her arms tightly round Miss Elliott's neck, the bright golden head reposed lovingly on her shoulder; the two were whispering their confidences together. "You must carry me up to bed," begged Florence, sleepily rubbing her eyes, and Dym rose obediently.

"You must say good-night to papa, Flossie," she whispered, and she held out the child to him as she spoke. Guy stooped over them both as he kissed Florence fondly; he shielded his eyes and watched her as she left the room, still carrying the child. What a young creature she looked! a small slight figure in a white dress, with a sweet, dark face that he had somehow grown to love.

She was not far off being very pretty, he thought to himself; there was such a tender, appealing look in her eyes sometimes, and the small shining head was set so daintily on her slim throat; how pleasant the touch of her hand had been to him when he had stood alone with her that wild March morning; but even as these thoughts flitted through his mind, there suddenly came before him the vision of another face—a grave beautiful face—with a broad low brow and solemn grey eyes that opened softly. "There was none like her; no wonder the angels claimed her so soon, she was too good for earth," he sighed. A moment after, when his mother spoke to him, he left the room, and no one saw the Squire's face again that night.

Dym never spent such a strange three days in her life. A sort of oppression and unreality was upon her. At times her conversation with Beatrix appeared a dream. Mrs. Delaire, when she met her next, seemed strangely subdued and treated her with marked kindness; it was true Dym did not respond to her advances, the girl was so sore of spirit that a word wounded her, she shrank away from the least approach to confidence on Mrs. Delaire's part, and confined herself entirely to the society of Mrs. Chichester and the child. She would sit for hours at her friend's feet, looking up at the blind, placid face as though she were learning how to take leave of it. Mrs. Chichester hardly knew what to make of her protégée's silence and sadness.

Dym only saw Mr. Chichester in the evening, and then he scarcely ever addressed her. Each day his face seemed to grow thinner and sadder. Dym's heavy heart grew heavier as she looked at him.

He must be hurt with her, after all—he was sorry she was going—he was sad, displeased. Poor Dym! There was no form of self-tormenting in which she did not indulge during those endless three days.

They came to an end at last.

Dym had been sent to the library on some trifling commission. Mr. Chichester was going out and wanted some papers copied—Guy never asked his cousin to do anything for him now—so Dym sat through the long afternoon accomplishing her task with her usual neatness and despatch till the last sheet was finished. She was still stooping over her work, when the Squire entered, bringing a current of fresh air with him.

"I am afraid I have set you too long a task," he said, looking over her shoulder. "How neatly you do this work, you would make a capital copying-clerk. Come to the fire and rest a little. I am sure both eyes and hands must be weary," and as Dym hesitated, he quietly added, "I want to speak to you," and Dym had no alternative but to obey. Mr. Chichester followed her and took up his old position. "My three days' grace has expired, I believe," he said, looking thoughtfully, not at her, but at the fire, " and you have a right to expect that our painful conversation should be renewed. Do you still persist in your former resolution, Miss Elliott?" turning on her so abruptly that Dym started, but she contrived to answer him with tolerable firmness.

"I have quite made up my mind to leave Ingleside and seek another situation."

"And you decline giving me your reasons?"

"I cannot—that is—I hoped you would understand that—you would not think me ungrateful, I mean," faltered Dym, growing white again.

"You need not fear misconstruction from me," he replied, calmly. "As far as I can judge of your motives, they do you infinite credit. My cousin has unfortunately raised a question that ought never to have been mooted, and I can well understand that you cannot remain here happily in your present capacity."

"I am glad you approve——" she began in a timid voice, and then stopped.

"Pardon me, I disapprove so strongly that I do not mean to let you go—if it be in my power to keep you—Miss Elliott," speaking now very gravely. "After what has passed there is only one way in which you can remain happily under my roof, and that is—do not be startled, my child—by becoming my wife."

"Mr. Chichester!" Dym rather breathed than said the words, her infinite surprise almost deprived her of utterance.

Mr. Chichester stood and watched her varying colour sadly, and then he came up to her and took her hand.

"I asked you to trust me. I have thought over it all; believe me this is the only way. Is the idea very repellent to you?" endeavouring to get a glimpse of her downcast face. But Dym hid all of it she could.

"No, oh no, but I am so unworthy," she whispered; "and then you do not love me, Mr. Chichester?"

"I have something to ask on the other side of the question. Do you think you could care for me, Dym?"

He had never called her by her name before, and the word thrilled her with incredible sweetness. Care for him! did she not love him so that her heart was nearly breaking within her?

She lifted her face, covered with burning blushes, as she strove to answer him. Something in the shy young face seemed to move Mr. Chichester strangely, for he suddenly drew it to him and kissed her brow.

"It is settled then; but, my child, I want you to listen to me for a moment. I will believe that you can care for me, grey-haired, middle-aged man that I am, whom trouble, and not years, have made hard and stern. But on my part I dare not deceive you. The best part of my life, my hopes, my love, is buried in Honor's grave."

She pressed his hand timidly—the kind hand

that had done so much for her and hers—he need not have told her that, she thought.

"You are so young that you have a right to expect an undivided heart. There are many men who would give you their best and truest love; I am not one of those, Dym."

"I know it," she whispered. "I do not expect it. I never dared hope for even this."

He smiled a little at the childish naïveté that betrayed so much: and then his tone resumed its gravity.

"When I lost Honor I lost the dearest thing earth had to offer me. I knew when she died I could never love any woman again as I had loved her. In some sense I am a broken-hearted man for life; but I think"—his voice changing into tenderness—"I should be a little less lonely if you will come to me, my dear."

And this from him. Dym was fairly weeping now.

"I have always loved my little friend dearly; she has come into my desolate home and made it pleasant to me. May I hope to keep her there always?"

No answer, only as his hand touched hers caressingly she suddenly stooped, and her girlish lips set the purest seal to her long love and fidelity.

"God bless you, my child. I will try to make you happy," were Guy Chichester's last words to her that night; and Dym's affection and loyalty found no fault with the sadness of the tone. Was she not his own—

did she not belong to him—her lord, her benefactor? Dym's tumultuous heart could find no room for doubt. With such thoughts as these she lay down to sleep that night, like a veritable child wearied out with over-much joy, and oblivious of the clouds of to-morrow.

## CHAPTER X.

### CRUEL AS THE GRAVE.

BEFORE they parted for the night Dym timidly sought permission from Mr. Chichester to share her secret with his mother, but she was a little surprised at the hesitation with which he acceded to her request. Her look of astonishment recalled him.

"You have promised to trust me," he said, with a grave smile at her perplexed face. "In fact you have given me a very full and convincing proof of your faith in me a very few hours ago. Am I asking too much if I beg you to trust me a little longer?"

"Do you wish me not to tell your mother then? I only thought——" Dym's perfect faith was jarring sadly with her old sturdy honesty. How was she to keep from Mrs. Chichester that she was engaged to her son?

Dym's face was always eloquent, and Mr. Chichester understood her thoroughly.

"You would be a very transparent deceiver, I am afraid. No, my child; I never meant to lay such a yoke on your conscience. Tell my mother by all means. I only ask that for a little while she may be the only confidante. Do you understand me?" taking her hand with one of his persuasive looks.

"Of course I shall do as you wish," she replied, colouring high under it. "There is no one else whom I care to tell, unless, perhaps, it were Humphrey," with a quick throb of pain as she thought how Will would have rejoiced in her happiness; and as though he again understood her, he drew her closer to him.

"I am almost glad that you have nothing to give up for me," he said tenderly after a minute's silence. "You have always seemed to belong to us somehow. My cousin is going away to-morrow to stay with some friends in Cumberland. On her return I shall tell her myself; but until things are definitely settled I have no wish that our affairs should furnish food for village gossip. Only," with a droll look, "I think with you that Humphrey has a right to know. I am afraid he wanted somebody very badly himself once upon a time. Would you rather he should hear it from me, Dym?" And Dym shyly answered "yes."

It was well that Dym was too young and inexperienced, as well as too humble-minded, to expect much attention from her fiancé, for certainly Mr. Chichester was not a demonstrative lover. Dym's unselfishness and devotion saved her from many a chill feeling of disappointment.

After a little time he resumed his ordinary manner with her, and except that he sought her society more frequently, and on all occasions paid the utmost deference to her opinion and wishes, there was nothing that could betray to the most watchful eyes that he had exchanged the friend for the lover.

A thorough understanding prevailed between them, but it could hardly be called courtship; he had always been kind and gentle with her, and now he was doubly so. With instinctive delicacy he contrived to infuse a new element of respect into his manner; he was less abrupt and more yielding. Dym was often distressed at the way in which he would set aside his own wishes or plans if he thought he could minister to her pleasure. A shadow of disrespect to Miss Elliott was sure to bring down his severest displeasure on the offender, tacitly rather than by word. He was proving to her that she was the woman whom the master of Ingleside delighted to honour, and yet was there nothing lacking in his devotion?

Dym thought her lover perfect; to her there was simply no flaw in her happiness. He was a little grave and absent in his manner perhaps when they were alone together, and yet Dym always felt that her presence soothed and pleased him. It never entered into the simple girl's heart to wonder why he spoke so little of their approaching marriage, but rather shunned the subject, as though it involved some present difficulty and pain. He would talk to her about herself, about Florence's future, and dwell long and gratefully on their mutual affection for the child; or else he would relapse into silence, and only by the rare caressing touch of his hand on her hair, would he show that he was conscious that she was still by him; and yet after a brief absence he would welcome her back so gladly that Dym knew that in some way she had become necessary to him.

But he never told her that he loved her, neither did he express a wish that she should call him by any other than the old name, "Guy." She said it sometimes softly to herself to see how it sounded, but somehow it never came naturally. "Perhaps when we are married he will teach me to say it," she thought. "I suppose he will not then be Mr. Chichester to me."

Dym bungled sadly when she began her story of her engagement to her friend. It was a pity no one was there to see the girl's sparkling blushing face. Before she had half finished she was clasped fondly in Mrs. Chichester's arms.

"I never dared to hope this," she sobbed. "Oh, my dear, you have made me so happy. Guy will never go away again now. I don't know how it is, Dym, but you have always been like my own daughter to me, but I shall love you all the better now." But Mrs. Chichester wisely kept her raptures for Dym, her womanly instinct led her to say very little to her son.

"I am glad of this, Guy," she said, detaining him by the hand when he came up to wish her good-night. "Very glad indeed; you could not have done better for yourself and Florence."

"I am sure of it for Florence," he returned briefly.

"Not for yourself, Guy?" in an anxious tone.

"For myself of course," with a light laugh. "Do you think I am capable of such a piece of self-sacrifice as that?"

Mrs. Chichester sighed.

"I know what this must be to you. Things are so different, and you have changed with them; but you will not refuse to let me wish you happiness, my son."

"No, indeed," he replied, speaking as though he were touched, and bending down to kiss her.

"It will not be unalloyed happiness just now, but it will come in time, Guy. It must, it will; she is so young, and loves you so dearly, you will make her what you will."

"She is a noble-hearted little creature, and I shall do my utmost to make her happy," was his reply in a tone of deep feeling, but as he dropped her hand Mrs. Chichester felt herself a little damped by his lack of enthusiasm.

"He has not forgotten Honor in spite of his new fancy," she thought; "Guy is so faithful." And she called Dym to her side and tenderly caressed the girl, as though she would make amends for some fancied slight.

Mr. Chichester kept his promise of telling Humphrey Nethecote. Humphrey came up to Ingleside one evening to wish her joy.

"The Squire has told me, my dear," he said, taking her two little hands, and looking at her fondly. "Somehow I have suspected this all along, Dym."

"O Humphrey, how could you?"

"It was not possible for him to see much of you and not love you," he returned in a voice that was a little husky: "it wouldn't be in man's nature, especially now he is so lonely and sad. Don't you feel that Honor will be glad to know you are taking care of him and the child?"

"Dear Humphrey, how good of you to say that," she whispered, with the tears in her eyes.

"Well, if he makes you happy, that is all I ask of him; you must not expect too much of him at first; the Squire is not the man he was, but he will pick up after a time. I should have guessed by your face something pleasant had happened. Folks will say you are young to be the Squire's sweetheart, when they see you beside him."

"He is not so old," she replied pointing; "Mr. Chichester is not quite forty yet—he told me so."

"Nay, but the trouble has changed him. Well, heaven bless you, my dear; when you are a happy wife you wont forget your old friend Humphrey?" somewhat wistfully.

"Never, Humphrey! What are you thinking about? Are you not our dearest friend—his as well as mine?"

"Nay, nay, not the dearest; but as true a one as you need have." And moved by the tender sadness of his expression, Dym, for the second time in her life, lifted up her face and kissed him.

The weeks passed on. April, with its chilly freshness and vaporous sunshine, was over, and the May hawthorn was filling the valley with sweetness.

Dym was getting used to her position now; the clear young voice could be heard again carolling among the shrubberies in the early morning; her light step had recovered its springy tread; the glow of a new hope shone in the clear dark eyes, and lit them with strange brilliancy. Guy would sigh softly to himself as he watched her about the house.

"She is so happy, that it would be cruel to shadow her brightness," he thought. "All I marvel is, that she can be so easily satisfied; she must feed on her own loving fancies. Sometimes I am afraid she will wake up and find I give her very little in return for her devotion; it is not always so with other men; the second love deadens the first to a great measure; they remember, but they are consoled. Will it ever be in her power to console me for Honor?"

And once this thought of his found utterance in words.

"What makes you look so happy, Dym?" he said once, when he found her singing to herself as she arranged the flower-vases. Dym blushed very prettily—she always did when he spoke to her—and then she mutely offered him a rose.

"Thank you, but I want the answer too," he said, detaining both the flower and the hand,

and looking at her with a sad sort of envy. Dym glanced at him shyly before she bethought herself of her reply.

"How can I help it," she said at last, "when you are so good to me?" Guy smiled at that.

"Am I good to you, my child? I am afraid you are not an impartial judge, Dym. What other girl of your age would be content with a sober middle-aged lover? Are you not afraid sometimes people will take you for my daughter?" pulling at his long grey beard with a comical gesture—people said his prematurely grey hair had aged Guy Chichester wonderfully. Dym treated him to one of her bewitching smiles in reply—they dazzled even him sometimes. In spite of what people might say, was he not always grand, lordly, altogether perfect, in her eyes? I believe Dym never could be persuaded that his beauty was not faultless; to her, her lover was a sort of Apollo and Jupiter Amnon in one.

"You are always good to me, except when you make these sort of speeches," she said, half pouting; "you are as bad as Humphrey, who is always making himself out a Methuselah. I would not have either of you a bit different. Don't you believe it?" looking up at him wistfully.

"I believe you are under some sort of glamour," he said, half seriously, half laughing. "There, put your hat on, my child; I want you and Florence to ride over to Ripley with me;" for Mr. Chichester had taught Dym to ride, and Humphrey

Nethecote had trained a pretty bay mare, and had sent it up to the Ingleside stables for Miss Elliott's special use.

The morning air was delicious, and Mr. Chichester in an unusually cheerful mood—nevertheless Dym did not entirely enjoy her ride.

"I am afraid you will be sorry to hear Beatrix is coming back to-morrow," Mr. Chichester had observed as he lifted her into the saddle. Dym stooped over her horse's neck and stroked its mane as she answered him. She was rather silent for the next mile or two, only Guy did not notice it; somehow those few words had damped her enjoyment. Mr. Chichester detained her for a few moments that night when his mother had left the room.

"Dym, I have never given you an engaged ring. I wonder you have not noticed the omission," he began when they were left alone.

"I thought you disliked the fuss," she returned timidly; "it was not necessary. Besides, people might be attracted, and we could trust each other without the sign-manual of our agreement."

"Ay," his keen brown face lighting up with one of his droll smiles, "you are a good little thing, and yet I always understood young ladies regarded such things as sacred talismans."

"Of course I should like one," returned Dym with her usual sweet honesty; "and your mother says——"

"Oh, my mother's taper fingers have been meddling, have they? Well, I have not forgotten you. Look here!" And he slipped a tiny hoop studded with pearl upon her finger. "Diamonds tell tales and so do emeralds. This is like yourself—simple, and pure, and good—and will keep its own counsel." Dym thanked him silently, but he did not let her go just yet.

"One word more, my child. You have reposed such generous trust in me that I feel I should be undeserving of it, if I did not show you more confidence in return. You know this time of year is full of painful memories to me; I shall breathe more freely when a month or two have passed. When the autumn sets in, I propose leaving Ingleside for a few weeks; my mother can then make our engagement public, and as soon as your arrangements are completed you can join me in London, where I propose our marriage being solemnized. You will not mind a quiet wedding away from Ingleside, will you, Dym?" And Dym trembling and flushing faltered out a happy "No."

It was the first time that he had ever alluded to their marriage. Alas! she little knew the difficulty with which he had braced himself to the subject. Delays were useless in their position; it would be better for them both when she was once his wife; he would be very fond of her, and take good care of her, and she would be the sunshine of the house, he thought—only Guy Chichester finished with a sigh.

Dym woke from happy dreams the next morning with a strange oppression at her heart—something had happened, or was going to happen. As her eyes fell upon the hoop of pearls she suddenly remembered Mrs. Delaire had fixed this evening for her return.

Dym scolded herself for being superstitious. Why did she always augur evil from Beatrix's visits? Her presence had often brought trouble to Dym, but surely now the spell must be broken.

Mr. Chichester had promised that he would announce their engagement to his cousin himself; it would be badly received, she knew. Dym had an instinctive feeling that Beatrix had always watched her with jealous eyes; she would regard her as a designing interloper, probably she would accuse her of intriguing. Would she meet her with cool sarcasm, or pour down the vials of her wrath on Dym's devoted head? Beatrix's envious passions were soon aroused, and on such occasions, as Dym well knew, her words could be dangerous.

Dym's lark-like voice was silent that morning; she was a little anxious and distrait at luncheon; Mr. Chichester noticed it.

"I am sorry we cannot have another ride together before Beatrix comes," he said as he joined Dym at the sunny terrace window. "But this stupid business of Latimer's obliges us to go over to York. I am afraid I shall not be back to dinner, mother, so you and Dym must do the best you can without me."

"Must you go?" sighed Dym. She followed him disconsolately out into the hall. When his horse was brought round to the door, as she looked up at him, he saw her eyes had tears in them.

"Why, my child, what ails you?" he asked in some surprise; for it was new to him to see a shadow on that bright face.

Dym drooped her head. "She did not know."

"I believe Beatrix has become a sort of moral wet blanket to us both," he said, cheerfully. "Never mind, you shall not be troubled with her long. Why, my dear Dym!" as she suddenly clasped her hands round his arm, and laid her face down upon them. Dym's timid reserve had never given way so completely, and Guy's tone was a little anxious.

"You have never been so sorry to part with me before," he said, trying to rally her. "I shall suppose all sorts of things. You must not make me too vain, Dym."

"It is not that," she returned, unsteadily. "I don't know why I want you so; but, oh, if only you need not go this afternoon?"

"You will make me wish it too, dear, if you look so sad about it. But, come, I cannot leave my little sunbeam eclipsing herself under such gloomy fancies; you must not send me off with that sort of face, Dym," as he lightly touched her forehead.

Dym gave him a misty smile at that. She slid a cold, nervous, little hand in his as she wished him good-bye. As he rode slowly down between the limes, he looked back and waved to her—a little shimmering grey figure, motionless in the sunlight.

Dym was alone in the drawing-room when

Mrs. Delaire arrived. Their greeting was a somewhat silent one. The young widow looked fatigued and depressed, and threw herself on the lounge with a wearied air. Her face had its jaded, dissatisfied expression. She was scarcely as beautiful as usual, Dym thought, and her tones had their old sharp ring.

"Miles tells me my cousin has ridden out this afternoon," she said, when Dym had relieved her of her mantle, and had brought her a cup of tea.

"Yes; he has been obliged to go to York with Mr. Fortescue. He has business in Harrogate, too; they will hardly be back till ten or eleven, Mr. Chichester fears."

"Mr. Fortescue generally chooses inconvenient times for business," retorted Mrs. Delaire; and there was another embarrassed silence.

Dym tried to talk on different subjects, but evidently Beatrix was not in a sociable mood. She listened with a preoccupied air, answered in monosyllables, and finally rose with a yawn.

"I am dreadfully tired; I think I had better go to Aunt Constance now. By-the-bye, Miss Elliott, Guy said nothing in his letters about your intention of leaving Ingleside."

"I—I have changed my mind."

"You are not going?" with a sudden hard inflection in her voice that set Dym's nerves quivering again.

"Mr. Chichester asked me to stay," she returned faintly, hanging down her head. What had become of Mrs. Chichester all this time? if only Florence would come into the room! Dym was starting away from the topic again in a sort of frightened way, but Mrs. Delaire sternly recalled her.

"My cousin asked you to stay?" she repeated, and her voice had a certain shrill tone in it. Surely she could not have heard aright. Ask Miss Elliott to stay, after what she had hinted—impossible. Guy could never have been guilty of such imprudence.

"If my cousin chose to be so rash, you need not have taken advantage of his generosity," she continued, coldly. "After what you have owned to me, it would be the grossest impropriety for you to remain under his roof."

"Stop! Mrs. Delaire; you must not speak to me in this way," interrupted Dym, beginning to tremble. Ought she to bear Beatrix's insolence now she belonged to him? She turned the hoop of pearl nervously round her finger as she spoke; the action did not escape Mrs. Delaire's sharp eyes.

"Why may I not speak to you? If you do not know what is fitting in your position, it is my duty to interfere and save you. Aunt Constance must know about this; I must tell her—warn her."

Beatrix was working herself up into a sort of passion now.

Dym humbled herself to make a final appeal.

"Mrs. Chichester knows. Why should you trouble yourself to interfere, Mrs. Delaire? I am doing you no wrong."

"How do I know that?" replied Beatrix—her eyes flashed; her bosom heaved stormily—"how do I know that you have not thrown yourself on his compassion; that you have not induced him to—— Who gave you that?" suddenly stretching out her hand in the attitude of a tragedy queen, and pointing to the poor little hoop of pearls.

"Pearls keep their own counsel," he had said to her; but there was no evading those jealous eyes.

Dym changed colour, and then womanly dignity came to her aid—evasion was impossible.

"Mr. Chichester gave me these," she said, looking up with calm eyes into Beatrix's excited face. "Now you know why you must not say these things to me; because—because I am going to be his wife."

Dym made her little confession very sweetly, but she was alarmed by its effect on Mrs. Delaire. The widow started as though she had received a shock; her pale face grew paler—she gasped for breath.

"To be his wife—Guy's wife—impossible! I will not believe it," she muttered, sinking on a seat. Then her mood changed.

"So this wise cousin of mine has proposed to you?" she went on, in a mocking, sarcastic voice that made Dym's cheek burn.

She bowed her head in assent.

"It is like him—Quixotic and mad as usual; and you, poor fool! you—you accepted him," in a tone of infinite contempt.

"I accepted him certainly, and we are engaged," returned Dym steadily.

Her quiet dignity seemed to provoke Beatrix beyond endurance.

"And this is your love and gratitude to your benefactor! Poor love—pitiable gratitude, I call it, Miss Elliott, to allow him to lower himself to such a sacrifice as that. But he shall not, if I can save him from it," stamping her slender foot as though the mere thought were insupportable to her. "You have acted so meanly, that I shall not try to spare you—ay, you may love him, Miss Elliott, but you will never be his wife. Girl as you are, you will shrink from the thought when I tell you Guy Chichester is only marrying you out of pity."

Dym's face grew almost convulsed. "How dare you—how dare you say that, Mrs. Delaire?"

"I dare to tell you the truth," replied Beatrix, scornfully. "Do you think he could ever choose such as you after Honor? What! you have lived under his roof all these years, and you have not discovered that Guy's weak generosity is his only fault? He is doing this for his mother's and his child's sake, and because he knows you love him."

"Oh, heavens! she has told him," cried the miserable girl, clasping her hands before her face.

"Yes, I told him," returned Beatrix, in the same freezing tone. "I would have kept it from him if I could, for I was afraid of this, but he made me angry and then it all came out. I told him you were leaving Ingleside because you were dying of love for him. Do you wish to hear how he answered me?" But Dym only wrung her hands and groaned heavily. In her darkest hour had she ever felt despair like this? Oh, God! that she should suffer such bitter shame and at the hands of this woman!

"He looked at me," went on Beatrix in the same hard voice, "as though I had dealt him a blow. 'Could you not have saved us both from this, Trichy?—could anything more unfortunate have befallen us all? Poor child, in whichever way I act I must wrong her. I could never love her as I love Honor—never, never!' You should have seen his face as he said it—it was pitiful—pitiful!"

"In mercy, and as you are a woman, hush!" Beatrix hardly recognised the voice. Her passion was dying out, and a sort of horror at her own work came over her as she looked at Miss Elliott. The girl was lying back in her chair with her eyes closed and her poor lips quite drawn and blue; it was as though she had heard her own death warrant.

"Are you faint—shall I get you something?" Beatrix was a mere girl still, an uncomfortable feeling of remorse began to take possession of her. Dym just stirred and shook her head; Mrs. Delaire watched her irresolutely.

Dym's dry lips were moving now; she signed to Beatrix to come closer.

"On your honour, is this true? As there is a heaven above us, have you not lied to me in this?" holding up her young hand solemnly with an appeal that was almost awful to Beatrix.

But it was too late to undo the mischief now.

"I have told you the truth," she returned, sullenly; "you must blame yourself, not me, for this miserable business."

"I shall try to forgive you some day, I suppose," faltered the poor child, "but not now—not now—the word would choke me," putting her hand to her head and looking at Beatrix in a bewildered sort of way. "Tell them I am not well—no one must come near me; I have work to do. I must think—think—think," with a ghastly smile that somehow curdled Beatrix's blood. As she walked from the room, Beatrix saw she put out a groping hand suddenly before her to steady herself.

She must think, this was her one idea—tears were useless, she must not grow faint. As she turned the key in the door of the little Grey Room which she still used as a dressing-room and sank down on the floor at the foot of her little bed, she told herself that she had work that would take all her strength to do; and a settled prayer resolved itself in her heart that she might have power to accomplish it.

Dym was not sinking under her misery, she was looking it in the face with a calmness that was akin to despair.

The evening sunshine flooded the terraces and gardens, and streamed in at the window till the grey dress was streaked with bars of gold;

the stars glimmered; the moon shone cold and clear; the night breezes stole into the darkened room, and still the crouching figure sat on with its face buried in its hands. Twice only it stirred. Once when they brought food to her door, and a feeble impatient voice had bade them set it down and go away, and again when verging towards midnight the clear sharp clang of the gate sounded in the distance, and firm footsteps drew nearer and nearer, pausing for a moment under her window and then passing rapidly round to the front entrance. As they died away Dym shivered, closed the window, and kindled a light.

She had thought it out, and now the time for her work had come.

"As there is a heaven above us have you not lied to me in this?" she had demanded solemnly of Beatrix; but even as she asked it she knew that the bitter truth had been told her.

He was marrying her out of pity—the man's vast tenderness, his chivalrous nature had prepared for her this degradation.

"Guy's weak generosity is his only fault: he is doing this for his mother's and his child's sake, and because you love him," Beatrix had said to her, and the ground had not opened and swallowed her in her shame.

No, she had not lied. Little by little the awful truth was stealing upon her. How white and drawn his face had looked in that twilight— that evening—when he had come to her and pleaded for three days' grace; how grave and passionless had been his voice as he wooed her;

with what settled sorrow he had told her that his heart was buried in Honor's grave!

Alas! she had thought that he had wanted her for his comforter—that he had found his hearth lonely, and craved for her woman's smile to brighten it. She would have been content with so little, she thought; she would have been satisfied with the merest crumbs of love. But that he should marry her out of pity! "Thank God, I will save him from that," she said, bitterly, as she trimmed her lamp.

Her slender preparations were soon made, and then she stole into Florence's room.

The child was sleeping peacefully, with one dimpled arm flung over the coverlet. Dym stooped down and kissed it softly. "Goodbye, my darling," she whispered as she turned away.

The first streak of dawn was stealing up the valley, and the pale line of light was widening behind the grey wall of Ingleside, when a little figure, veiled and cloaked, came slowly down the terrace, with the faithful collie following it.

At the lodge gates they paused.

"You must not come any further with me, Kelpie," and as he licked her hand irresolutely she knelt down on the ground and hugged the dog to her bosom. "Oh, good old Kelpie, dear Kelpie, go back to him; you must not forsake him too." And her tears streamed over the rough coat and shaggy paws of her faithful companion.

Five minutes after that the heavy gate had

clanged between them. Guy heard it, and muttered drowsily to himself as he turned in his sleep.

"Good-bye, dear happy Ingleside; good-bye for ever," she moaned as she turned away, and the echo in her own heart went on ceaselessly, "For ever."

## CHAPTER XI.

A SHADOW ON THE WALL.

"WHERE is Miss Elliott this morning?" were Guy Chichester's words as he entered the breakfast-room.

Beatrix, who was pouring out the coffee, bent her head over the silver urn, and feigned not to hear the question, but she listened a little anxiously to Stewart's answer.

"No one has seen Miss Elliott, sir. Dorothy —that is, Phyllis—did say to Miles that her young lady must be ill or something, for she hasn't been near Miss Florence since last evening."

Mr. Chichester made no reply; he even checked Flossie when she seemed disposed to burst into some childish confidence.

"Go on with your breakfast, Flo," he said, a little irritably, as the child looked up eagerly. "Trichy, if you have done with Stewart I should like him to fetch me the *Times* from the station. Dison has forgotten to send it." And as soon as the servant was out of hearing, he continued in a low voice to his cousin, "Isn't it singular, Trichy, the child will have it that Miss Elliott never went to bed at all? She declares she came to her in the middle of the night with her bonnet and cloak on, and kissed her, and said she was going away. What could have put such nonsense into the child's head, I wonder?" But in spite of his impatient tone, Guy looked anxious and perturbed.

Beatrix changed colour. "Of course she must have been dreaming, Guy. Children have such strange fancies. Most likely Miss Elliott is taking an early walk; she complained of headache when I arrived yesterday."

"She was perfectly well when I left her," returned Mr. Chichester, uneasily. "Miles told me she was not at dinner last night. I hope nothing unpleasant passed between you, Trichy?" he added, with one of his searching glances. Beatrix was paler than usual—even her cousin noticed her embarrassment. The servants' comments had already reached her ears, she knew from Phyllis that Miss Elliott's bed had not been slept in.

Beatrix drew herself up a little haughtily as Mr. Chichester spoke, but he did not repeat his question; during the rest of the meal he sat in thoughtful silence, and as soon as it was over he left the room and went straight to the library.

His hand was on the bell, when the gleam of something white on his writing-table attracted his eye, and he looked up eagerly—it was a note in Dym's handwriting.

As he opened it and the pearl hoop dropped at his feet his face expressed bewilderment, almost alarm; but a grave, pitiful look came into his eyes as he read and re-read the few blotted sentences, and once he sighed heavily, " Poor child, poor little wounded heart!" he muttered. " Cruel, cruel!" and then his face grew dark and stern again.

" Oh, my dear, my dear, how could you have done it?" she wrote. " If I could have loved you more I must have done it now that I know all your noble goodness. To think that after her you could stoop to me; that you could put aside your own grief to try and comfort me, poor little humble me!

" O my darling, forgive me if I call you that once, I never shall again—think how I must love you when I tell you I am going away without even wishing you good-bye to save you from such a sacrifice. She has told me all: it was generous, it was like you, but why, why did you think such noble self-devotion was necessary? You have wronged me, dear, you have indeed, but you did not mean to be cruel.

" If I had left you I should have gone on loving you all my life. I am not ashamed of owning that now—why should I be? You have always been so grand—so noble in my eyes; and then one day, when you were old, and Florence had left you and you wanted me, I would have come to you and been your faithful nurse and friend, and you would have been glad to see me— I know you would have been—and then this miserable mistake would not have occurred.

"But you must not be unhappy about it, or think I have acted impulsively in leaving you. I could not be your wife now, dear, could I? The very thought humbles me. Tell your mother all, she will understand and be sorry for me; and ask my darling Flossie not to fret. And now God bless you. I know He will. He will not be angry with me for leaving you so, and you must not be.

"Your faithful and loving friend,

"Dym."

Beatrix was still sitting at the deserted breakfast-table when her cousin's step sounded in the passage, and a moment after he entered.

She knew what was coming, almost before he had turned the handle of the door. Some subtle instinct warned her that he meant to overwhelm her with his reproaches. Had she gone too far—had she in her sudden madness of jealousy miscalculated this girl's influence; could it be that he loved her after all—that it was really his desire to make her his wife? Beatrix was by no means devoid of courage, nevertheless her heart died within her when she saw his face.

"Don't, Guy! Whatever has happened you must not blame me," she said, almost cowering away beneath that dark wrathful look. Bold as she was, how was she to confront him in his sternness—would her pride carry her through such an ordeal? "Indeed, indeed, it was not my fault," she continued, pitifully.

"Read that," was his only answer, as he took

the folded paper from his breast and laid it before her. "Do not sully your lips with falsehood, Beatrix," he continued, with a slight accent of scorn, "I know exactly what passed between you as though I had heard your every word. Oh, Trichy, Trichy," his voice breaking with sudden emotion, "I could almost find it in my heart to hate you for this, that you—you, of all people, should have wrought me this deadly wrong."

"I did not say much—I did not indeed, Guy," she returned humbly. His anger was dreadful to her. Would she not have died to win one word of love from his lips? and now he was filling her cup to the bitter brim with his righteous scorn. "It was only a word I let fall by accident; she provoked me, she often does, Guy—indeed you do not know Miss Elliott as well I do. You must not be angry because I think she is not worthy of you—she has deceived you, as she has deceived others, with her artful ways."

"Take care, Beatrix," he interrupted, menacingly. His eyes flashed, and it was only by a strong effort he controlled himself. "Take care," he repeated more quietly, "you are speaking of my future wife. Another such word as that and I shall be constrained to bid you see my face no more."

"Your wife!" gasped Beatrix, and some deadly suppression of feeling turned her lips white. "But she has gone—Miss Elliott has gone."

"You have driven her away for a little space," he replied, in the same hard voice; "but I am still bound to her; whenever she will she may come back, and find her place ready for her, for I swear no other woman shall be my wife."

"Guy, Guy!" But Beatrix's agonized exclamation was unheeded; he had turned away from her with that terrible look still on his face, and in another moment she was alone.

Before the next hour had elapsed Humphrey Nethecote had been summoned to the Squire's library, and for a long time the two men were closeted together.

"You may telegraph your success. If I do not hear before to-morrow night I shall follow you," were the Squire's parting words. "Be prudent—do nothing to compromise her or me, and above all do not let her suspect that her movements are watched.

"Let me only know she is safe—that must do for the present. We must leave her free, Humphrey. The mischief is done, and cannot be undone without time and patience."

"Oh, oh, plenty of that needed for a snarl of the devil's making. Take my advice, Squire, and get rid of that woman; she was never to my mind, nor to poor Honor's either."

"I must leave that to my mother," returned Guy, with a touch of haughtiness. "I am going up to her room now. Poor dear, she will fret more than any of us. Promise to be wary, Humphrey, for both our sakes," he continued, wringing Humphrey's hand, and then he went slowly and heavily back into his own room.

Humphrey gave a queer little satisfied grunt,

when he was left alone, which accorded strangely with the perplexed look of pain his face had hitherto worn.

"It is an ill gait, but it may end better than we thought," he muttered, as he descended the hill, "that is if it be not the death of her. Poor child, she little suspects the heartache she has caused, the Squire would rather have cut off his right hand than this had happened; he'll be blaming himself and thinking more of her in consequence. If she had had the wisdom of the serpent instead of the harmlessness of the dove, she could not have done better for herself than going away and leaving him to miss her," and the old pain tugged at Humphrey's heartstrings as he thought how dearly and truly Guy would learn to prize his treasure.

"Be you going to Lunnon, Farmer Nethecote?" was Dison's astonished greeting, as Humphrey made his appearance on the high windy platform.

"Oh, eh, we country folk must be having our sight-seeing sometimes," returned Humphrey, absently; "yours must be a dull kind of place, Dison; how many passengers do you book an hour, I wonder, and what makes you think I am going to London, Dison, when my ticket is for Harrogate?"

"Folks like you and t' Squire aren't over fond of putting up at Harrogate," returned Dison, with a grin. "Why, when I see t' Squire's black bag I say, 'Lunnon, for sure.' Why, you've a bag yourself, Farmer Nethecote, and it ain't samples nor market-day."

"You are a sharp one, Dison," returned Humphrey, trying to speak jocularly, but with an uneasy flush on his honest face. "These Harrogate trains are as unpunctual as ever, I see; our ladies complain sadly when they are out on a shopping expedition and get home late for dinner."

Dison grunted unintelligibly by way of answer. Slowness of traffic was a sore subject with him.

"Miss Elliott will be back in plenty of time, I should think," he answered, crossly. "It is early birds as pick up worms, as I thought to myself when I served her with her ticket. To think of one of the Ingleside ladies taking the first train! She was asking after my wife at the time, and I never heeded; she asked for a single instead of a double; she'll be finding out her mistake, I'll be bound, before she reaches Hampswaite."

"Oh, the best of us are absent sometimes," returned Humphrey nervously, as he moved away a step from the garrulous stationmaster. Dison had been in the Squire's service before his brother-in-law had entered it, and was well acquainted with all the doings at Ingleside.

As the train appeared in sight he heaved a sigh of relief. "There's not a doubt but I am on her track," he muttered, as he stepped into the second-class compartment. "After all, the Squire's right, and she has gone back to the old place."

Little did Dym guess as she took her weary journey from Harrogate to York, and from York to London, that her faithful friend Humphrey was following in her footsteps.

Guy's unerring instinct had not been at fault; sick and bewildered, almost numb from intensity of pain, yet never faltering in her purpose, Dym watched the flying milestones diminish between her and London, and while Humphrey was trying to beguile the longest hour he had ever known on the ramparts at York, Dym was dragging herself slowly up the steps of the old house in Paradise Row.

"Richard, Richard, here is our young lady come back," but Susan Maynard's joyous exclamation changed into one of alarm as Dym tottered into the dusky passage and almost fell into her arms. "Quick, husband, quick, she is going to faint; oh, whatever has come to my darling dearie that they have sent her back to us like this?"

"I am not going to faint, I am only so tired," but Dym's explanation was choked by a sudden sob; she cast a bewildered look round the little room, and then at the faces of kind Richard Maynard and his wife. "Where am I? Where is Will? What has happened to me?" cried the poor child, stretching out her hands to them. A moment afterwards she had thrown her arms round Susan's neck, and was crying out to them hysterically to keep her—to hide her somewhere for the dear love of Heaven; her heart was broken, and no one wanted her; she would die soon and go to Will.

Oh, if she could only die! That was the one

rebellious prayer that rose to her lips morning, noon, and night, during those first few weary days that followed her flight from Ingleside; and, indeed, the girl's sick despair filled her humble friends with dismay and pity.

She had had a great sorrow, and had left Ingleside for ever, that was all she told them; but before many hours were over they were in possession of the truth.

"We will watch over her as though she were our own—as though she were little Dick himself," broke out Richard huskily, as Humphrey, in an agitated voice, prayed them to be gentle with her, and as he wrung their hands at parting, Susan sobbed out, "Richard's not the man he was since our Dick has gone, but he'll keep his word; you may trust him, sir. Tell your Squire we will guard her like our own daughter."

Dym, lying on her bed, or pacing the room restlessly, little thought of Humphrey's grave whispering under the stars. Once, as she approached the window and drew back the curtain, the sound of footsteps on the pavement below caused her to drop it hastily. The little group broke up somewhat hurriedly after that, and Dym came back and rested her head against the low window sill. The starlight somewhat soothed her; it made her think of Will and the great cloud of witnesses.

"O Will, are you sorry for me? Do you know how I suffer?" she would say, half aloud, over and over again.

Susan would have guessed the girl's secret

even if Humphrey had not imparted it. Dym would start from her sleep with broken exclamations and snatches of words, the bursting forth of a long pent up agony. "He is doing this for his mother's and his child's sake, and because he knows you love him," Susan heard her say one night, when the girl's restless moaning had called her from her bed. "Was it wrong to love you; is it wrong now; how can I help it? oh, my darling, my darling, when I must love you to my life's end!" And as Susan stooped over and soothed her she broke into passionate weeping, and faltered out between her sobs "that she was very young still, and had no mother; only Will knew, her dear Will; and only he would believe her, that she never meant to harm them like this."

But even in her intolerable desolation, when the memory of all she had lost came upon her, and the prospect of her loveless life filled her with intense loathing, even then she never blamed Guy Chichester.

He had stooped to her out of his nobleness; his very goodness had prepared for her this humiliation; out of pity he had chosen her to be his wife; a wife uncrowned, unadorned by her husband's love. Dym's cheeks would flame with sudden hot pain as the remembrance of the last few weeks flashed before her. Good heavens, how happy she had been! the very sound of his voice in her ear, the touch of his hand on her hair had filled her with silent ecstasy; his caresses had been few; but she had never complained of their coldness; his silence had been more perfect to her than another man's words. Absorbed in her worship she had feasted and been satisfied with a few crumbs of human kindness; but she could not stoop to his pity.

"I could have married you, Guy," she whispered. "I could marry you now; but I should scorn myself for doing it. If you had only wanted me a little; oh, ever so little, dear, I would never have left you; but to make me your wife out of pity——" and her head dropped forward on her breast as Beatrix's cruel words rose to her memory.

But there were times when her yearning would be too great for even her endurance, when she would feel as though she must go back just to look upon the walls of Ingleside, and to satisfy herself that he and the child were well. If she could only see their faces for one moment; if she could hear his voice once more, and knew that he was not angry with her, she could have borne her misery more bravely; but the utter silence that had fallen between them seemed to the unhappy girl almost like the silence of death.

"He knows where I am; he could seek me out, or send me one word—one word—to assure me of his forgiveness," she said, with the strange contradiction and argument of sorrow. "He is hurt or grieved, or perhaps my sudden flight has angered him; and yet it is not like him to be so hard when he knows—when he must know—how I love him," and the tears rolled down her pale cheeks and fell into her lap. Suffering—the sting and uncertainty of her trouble—was killing her; the dull numb pain at her heart never left her day or night; a feverish restlessness throbbed in her pulse; she grew white and weak, almost to illness; but not for this would she spare herself.

"I must go out and work; if I stay in here and brood over my troubles I shall go mad," she said one evening, sliding a hot hand into Susan's and looking up in her face with heavy lustreless eyes; but Susan would not help her young lady.

"Work! you're just fretting yourself into sickness, that is what you are, dearie. Here's Richard says you're pining yourself into a shadow, and no wonder when you eat nothing and can't sleep for sorrowful thoughts. Work! there is not a day's work in you left," continued Susan, indignantly.

Dym smiled faintly at her vehemence.

"If I stay here and think, of course I shall be ill," she persisted, gently. "Dear Susan, don't you see how bad it must be for me? I cannot take another situation, not just yet. I have money enough to last me for a long time; but tell me of some one Will used to know; let me try and help others who are as miserable as myself."

Did she remember who beside Will had worked at St. Luke's. Once Richard Maynard mentioned in her hearing the name of a labourer living in the adjoining street who had met with an accident.

"They say it will cripple him; it is that Bill Saunders that used to be the plague of Mr. Elliott's life. He was one of Latimer's lambs as they called him. Mr. Latimer had rare work with him.

"Where does he live, Richard?" asked Dym, eagerly. A faint spot of colour came into her cheeks; her hands moved restlessly. As soon as it grew dark she tied on her bonnet and hurried round to the sick man's dwelling. "They say I be crippled for life," groaned poor Bill, looking into the sympathizing face that bent over him; "and there be Nancy and the children, and who is to put bread into their mouths?"

"I will take care of them; don't be afraid, Bill. If the doctor says your leg must come off, you must make up your mind to part with it like a man; God will take care of Nancy and the children, and I mean to be your friend." Dym spoke with a little flurry and haste; but Bill thought he had never heard so sweet a voice.

Susan gave a little cry of surprise when Dym glided softly back in the moonlight; the eager colour had not yet faded out of her cheeks; she looked up in Susan's face with a smile sweet almost to sadness, her voice had a quaver in it of mingled sorrow and joy.

"He is in great pain, but I do not think he will die; we must pray that he will not for his poor wife's sake. Look here, Susan," and Dym opened her mantle, and there nestled closely at her breast lay a little child.

"It was such a little creature," cried the girl, softly, "and the mother was so worn out with the others, and it feel asleep in my arms, and I thought I would carry it home and take care of it for a little while;" and her voice suddenly breaking, "They called it Florence."

Somehow under the dark eaves of the houses in Paradise Row a sigh answered Dym's words—low as they were they had been overheard. God bless her for the thought; was she thinking of him as well as the child?

Little did Dym guess who stood outside in the June moonlight, that only a few yards of narrow road divided her from Guy Chichester.

People marvelled at the grave bearded figure that stood so long and silently before the humble house. The window was opened, through the screen of plants he could see the soft halo of lamplight, a moth wheeled round it; there was the low chair, the girlish figure in the grey gown he remembered so well; the gentle bent head still stooping over the child in her lap.

What a grave face it had grown! was it fancy or the lamplight? or did it grow suddenly pale, and the lips quiver? What was that sudden mist that blotted it out from his sight, as he turned hurriedly away and strode through the silent streets? Because he has heard a whisper that will haunt him through many a lonely day.

"For his mother's and his child's sake—O Flo, darling Flo, I dare not—he would not ask it now."

Few men would have envied the feelings of

Guy Chichester as he paced through the midnight streets; some unaccountable sadness and longing had drawn him from his home; some chivalrous instinct impelled him to traverse those weary miles that he might see her with his own eyes, and judge for himself that others were tending her well.

But he never meant to speak to her; her refuge should be sacred from him and his. He thought the time was not come yet that he should dare to plead his cause with her.

"I could not be your wife now, the very thought humbles me." Good heaven, to think how he had failed in his sacrifice; he had meant to shield her with his strong arm, to make her young life a very joy to her, and she had fled from him crushed and broken-hearted.

He had told his cousin that he was bound to her, and that no other woman should be his wife. He had sworn it with a blackness of brow that had been dreadful to her; but how was he to win for himself the girlish purity that refused to become an unloved wife.

Did he love her—could he ever love her—as he had loved Honor? The heart of his heart—his very soul—as he had once in his madness called her. Could any other woman, the best, the noblest, replace the bride of his youth—the mother of his child? He dare not lie to himself; he knew such a thing was impossible; even in his brief sad wooing he had bidden her remember that the best of his life was buried in Honor's grave. No, he did not love her—not as men should love when they seek to gather some young life into their own. For his mother's and child's sake he had wooed her, and because her presence had rendered his hearth less desolate. How was she to know that a growing tenderness was springing up in his heart for her, and that he was longing for her with a soreness that surprised himself?

How the sweetness of her presence had comforted him! Ah, he knew that now. How meekly and quietly she had borne her honours as the future mistress of Ingleside. Her unselfishness, her devotion to his child, had inspired him almost with reverence, and yet with him she had carried herself as humbly as a child.

"You have always been so grand, so noble in my eyes," she had said to him once, and he could feel the soft touch of her little hand as she had timidly stolen it into his in the twilight. At a word of praise from him her dark eyes would shine like stars, and her face would be covered with blushes. "You are my king, I must serve you always," she had whispered once as she performed some little womanly office, and he had smiled in his sad way and let it pass.

Ah, he knew well how she loved him, the very sense of his power over her made him shrink in very delicacy from taking an undue advantage. "If I go to her and tell her that I want her, that my home is lonely, and my heart heavier than ever without her she will come to me— I know she will—but I shall not make her happy. If only some chance would bring us together, and I could tell her that her place is ready for her, and that I want my little friend to be always near me, I think she would come and cling to me as she clung that last time ; and perhaps I might teach her to trust me once more." And again the mist swam before his eyes as he remembered how that evening he had ridden slowly between the lines, and had seen her standing, a little shimmering grey figure, motionless in the sunlight.

So Guy Chichester went back to Ingleside and worked hard, and rode, and played with his child, and talked with his faithful friend Humphrey; but ever as he sat alone or paced the moonlight terraces, one picture rose before his eyes—the figure of a girl with a dark sweet face and shining head, bent over a sleeping child.

" ' It is such a little creature, Susan,' he could hear her say, ' and it fell asleep in my arms, and they called it Florence.' Come hither, Flo, my darling. Do you love papa or auntie best now? What, auntie still? Hush, don't cry, my child, auntie will come back to us soon."

The June days had worn heavily away and then July and August, and the humble folk in Paradise Row began to whisper and shake their heads as Dym's slight figure came down the hot sunny streets. "She has a purely white kind of wasting look," one of them was saying to Susan Maynard; "that's how my Willie was took— fretted and pined himself into his grave—she has a look like Mr. Elliott's when he was rarely bad."

"It is the mind wearing on the body, that's what it is, neighbour," returned Susan, lifting her apron to her eyes. She had been shedding tears recently; but she wiped them now hastily away, as her young lady came wearily down the street.

"Am I late, Susan? are you looking for me? Poor little Robert was so near his end that I waited till all was over; he died so happily, Susan."

"You look every bit as bad as him," returned Susan, in a vexed tone; "not a speck of colour in your face. You'll not take it to heart, will you, my darling dearie—you'll be good and brave even if there is more coming to trouble you?" she continued in a caressing voice, as she drew Dym gently into the passage.

"It did not trouble me, dear little Robert was so glad to go; he said a prayer so prettily—oh, what is that?" as a dark shadow fell against the narrow entry.

"It is only Mr. Nethecote, you will be good and brave, dearie?"

"Yes, it is only I," said Humphrey, coming forward and holding out his hand—his face had a grave sadness on it; his great hand trembled as Dym's little fingers clung to it. "I have come to fetch you, my dear; the Squire wants you—we all want you. We fear he is dying."

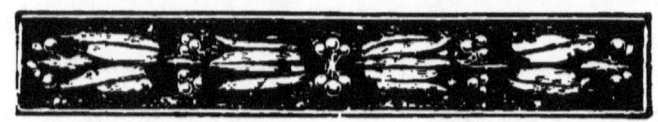

## CHAPTER XII.

#### THE LAST OF THE COBWEBS.

T is impossible to describe Dym's feelings as Humphrey delivered himself of his sorrowful message.

"It seems I am always to be the messenger of evil tidings to you, my dear," he said, tremulously.

It was hard on him; why was he ever constrained to give her pain? his heart throbbed with great pitiful beats as he watched the girl's silent anguish. She had uttered a low glad cry of recognition at the sight of her friend; but now she stood white and stricken, clinging to the fond hand that had dealt her this second blow.

"Hush, it is God's will; if it comes we must try to bear it."

"Is it God's will? it is not true. He cannot mean that surely," exclaimed the poor child; her hand closed round Humphrey's almost convulsively; an awful pallor came over her face; a powerlessness that was not faintness seemed creeping over her; her heart felt like a stone in her bosom; she was stifled, suffocated.

"Oh, it is not true, I cannot bear it," came

in a hoarse cry, almost a shriek, from her lips. Was this the end of her love and faithfulness? Guy, her Guy, for whom she would have laid down her life, dying!

"Hush, my dear, hush!" cries Humphrey with a sob. Sick and dizzy she had turned from him and had sunk, nay, almost fallen, into Will's chair. Humphrey watched her as she lay with her head flung back on the horsehair cushion till his honest heart was almost broken, her face looked almost as grey and drawn as the dead man's had done. "Oh my child, hush! they think so, but doctors are often wrong; we will not lose hope, you and I," he said, leaning over her with tears in his eyes and stroking the cold little face with his great hands. Dym's feeble fingers suddenly stopped him.

"There is hope, then? everything is not lost?" she said, half rising in her hysterical agitation. "Oh, Humphrey, you might have killed me," pushing her hair from her face and looking at him with wild pathetic eyes that stabbed him afresh.

"Nay, nay, Dym—it was my clumsiness: it seems no good beating about the bush when there is bad news to be told—and it is bad enough, God knows. When they brought him in, more than one of us thought it was all up with the Squire."

"You have not told me, Humphrey—was it an accident, then?" cried Dym, faintly; the numbness was creeping on her again.

"Ay!" he replied slowly, drawing the cold hands into his own to warm them. Dym shivered and hid her face, as bit by bit he imparted the terrible news—a whole world of horror and doubt lay in Humphrey's succinct narrative. Guy had been trying a new mare that he lately purchased—a beautiful creature, but vixenish and wild-blooded, and almost as uncontrollable as an unbroken colt.

"I had warned him against her, my dear," Humphrey had explained in his mild way; "but you know the Squire, when he has got an idea in his head. The mare was his last new hobby, and nothing would do but he must break her in himself." No one knows how it happened; something—a shot from the plantation—startled the animal; but she reared, lost her balance; and before the Squire could get his foot out of the stirrup, she fell backward on him."

"Humphrey," cried the girl, starting up in a sudden agony, "you are not keeping anything from me—he is not dead?"

"Nay, nay; things are bad enough without making them worse; he has some of his ribs broken, for she rolled right over him, and they say one arm is injured; but it is the head, Dym! they fear congestion of the brain. It is three days ago, but he has only spoken once, and that was to ask for you."

"And when was that?"

"Last night; that is why I am here now."

"Why are we waiting, then? we are losing time. If we should be too late! Oh, Humphrey, take me to him," clasping her hands round his arm.

"Of course I will take you to him; what else have I come for?" returns Humphrey in a slow kind voice, that somehow soothes the girl's agitation.

She laid back passively after that, and let Susan make her little preparation.

"Good-bye; Humphrey will take care of me," she said, smiling sadly into the faithful creature's tear-stained face, as she drew down her veil, and sank into the corner of the carriage.

"You must try not to fret, Dym; while there is life there is hope," Humphrey said once, trying to rouse her.

Dym's head dropped upon her breast, but she made no answer. Would that weary journey ever end, the girl wondered? She could hardly have borne it but for Humphrey's kindness. Dym was so utterly spent that she could only thank him with faint smiles. She swallowed the wine he brought her at York, but she could not eat; some choking oppression lay at her heart. Her ghastly looks alarmed Humphrey. Would the flying milestones ever lessen? Would they be too late, after all? And then came the sickening thrill of recognition—there was Birstwith at last!

"They have sent up the waggonette; he is not worse, Dym."

Humphrey talked fast and eagerly as he hurried Dym along the little platform. There was Disan, touching his hat officiously; there were Stewart and the bays waiting for them.

Dym drew down her veil more closely as they

dashed through the village. Every one would know her of course. There was the mill, and the weir; the boys were splashing barelegged among the boulders as usual; there was the Nidd rippling with streaks of silver through the trees; there was the church and the Vicarage; the lodge gates had opened and closed after them, and they were whirling through the shrubberies. Grey-headed Miles was waiting at the hall-door, and then Humphrey came round and lifted her out.

"Go into the drawing-room; I must find Mrs. Chichester," he whispered; but Dym lingered. "Don't keep me from him, however he is. I will be good; you know I will, Humphrey," she implored; but Humphrey's only answer was a reassuring smile, and he was turning away, when Florence suddenly ran in from the dark hall, and flung herself upon Dym.

"Oh, Flo! Flo! my darling Flo!" cries Dym, with a sudden sob, as the child nestles delightedly in her arms. "Have you wanted me, Flo?"

"Naughty auntie, to go away," returns Florence, with a shower of sweet kisses, that seem to cool the girl's hot brain.

"No, you are not to cry; Grannie is crying now, and all because papa is better. Yes, papa is better, and Grannie says so; and you are to come to her now at once."

"Courage Dym," says Humphrey, with the same kind smile; but all the same he has almost to support her under this new dizziness. Better! what is there mercy in heaven for them even now? She goes up the staircase panting and breathless with the child still clinging to her.

"Oh, my dear! my dear! God has been good to us. He has slept! he is better."

Dym never knew what answer she made. She heard Humphrey say, "Thank God!" devoutly, as though he were in church. She heard Florence exclaim, "How white auntie looks! poor auntie!"

"Leave her to me, Humphrey: I know what it is," says Mrs. Chichester, gently.

Yes; he thinks he may leave them safely now, as he sees the two women clinging together. He knows the girl's tortured brain will relieve itself in tears on her friend's bosom.

"He is saved—they do not fear for his brain now. Oh, Dym, is it not Goodness itself watching over us? My boy is spared to his mother—spared to us both."

"Hush! I am content, though it be only to you. Can you not understand that?" interrupted the girl, flushing and paling, as the blind face bends tenderly over her. "Oh, I have been wicked; I have almost died of it," she whispered, covering her face with her hands; "and now this has happened to punish me for my selfishness. Dear, dearest, I can be happy now, though his life is only spared for your sake," kissing the wrinkled hand as she spoke.

"You are my own little daughter, whatever he makes you," was the fond reply; "Dym, you must never leave me again. I cannot do without you. I think he has wanted you badly

16—2

too, though he has never said so until last night."

"No, no," almost panted the girl; "you must not talk so; it is not right; and he lying there brought back to his mother and child from the very gates of death."

Mrs. Chichester smiled as she put her hand fondly on the bowed head. Dym's tears still flowed, but her pale face was radiant. He would not die; he wanted her; he had asked for her; she should see him again. Dym's simple loyalty could go no further than this; more would have dazzled and overcome her, but now she was content.

She would see him; she would nurse him. He had forgiven her, and would be her friend again; here was matter for rejoicing. She acquiesced without regret when she heard he had taken his sleeping draught, and that she must not see him that night. She laid down in her little bed spent and worn out by conflicting emotion, and even in the midst of her *Te Deum* fell into a heavy dreamless sleep.

It was not until the afternoon of the next day that Dym was admitted to the sick-room. She had been wandering about her old haunts, hand in hand with Florence, trying to beguile the feverishness of waiting, and was looking pale and worn, when Humphrey came in search of her.

"You may come now, Dym; he has been asking for you several times, but he looked feverish, and we thought it better to wait. You must be quiet, and soothe him if he speaks; it is early days, and we must be careful still, Dr. Grey says."

"Yes, I know," was Dym's hardly audible answer, as she prepared to obey Humphrey's summons. Kelpie was lying at the door of the sick-room, a sudden mist swam before her eyes, as she stooped to caress him.

It was a close sultry afternoon, and the windows had been flung open that the air might refresh the invalid. Mrs. Chichester sat beside the farthest one; her knitting had fallen into her lap, and on the bed lay the motionless figure, high up on the pillows, with one bandaged arm resting on the coverlid.

At Dym's hesitating footstep it stirred slightly, and a smile passed over the pale face.

"At last, my child; you have come at last," Dym heard in the old well-known voice.

"Oh, Mr. Chichester!" Dym could say no more, as Guy Chichester stretched out his uninjured arm, and drew her gently towards him, trembling from head to foot, and hardly able to refrain from tears.

"Sit down; no, you must not stand. Poor child, it has gone hardly with you I see; Dym, are you so sorry for me?" his own eyes moist, as he saw her emotion.

"It might have been your death; hush, you must not talk, indeed you must not, Mr. Chichester;" Dym in her agitation is unconscious that her tears are falling now on the hand that still holds hers.

"Are those tears for me? Oh, my child, I do

not deserve them," he whispered, lifting the little hand to his lips. " Dym, have you any idea how I have wanted my little friend ?"

" She is here now," was the unsteady answer.

" Yes she is here, thank God! Dear, you are right ; I must not talk much, my head is not to be trusted, you will not leave me again, my child?"

" Not while you want me," returned Dym, unconscious of any meaning attaching to his words ; his smile mystified her.

"That is well ; one day I shall remind you of your promise," he replied in a voice so faint, that Dym forgot her agitation—everything—in the desire to relieve his evident suffering.

Before many hours were over Dym found herself installed in the sick-room ; the mother could only sit helplessly beside her son's bed, the brunt of the nursing fell on Dym and Humphrey. Humphrey was strong and helpful, but Dym's tender ministries were most grateful to Guy Chichester, lying sore and bruised and in secret anguish of pain ; he suffered less when Dym dressed his injured arm ; her cool skilful manipulations afforded him comparative ease ; by the unerring instinct of love she guessed his wishes ; the cooling drink was at his lips, and the fragrant water laving his burning head before he had shaken off the indolence of weakness sufficiently to frame them in words.

" How good you are to me! have you found your true vocation now ?" he whispered once as she stooped over him to turn the heated pillow, and he looked at her a moment with something of his old drollery. Dym turned away without answering, but her colour rose; it seemed to her half a lifetime ago since that talk in the little room in Paradise Row, when the tall bearded stranger had watched her from Will's chair with grave quizzical eyes, and had told her that nursing and not teaching was her vocation, and she had answered him with girlish vehemence.

"Come here, my child; have I hurt you?" and there was a wistful look in the dark eyes as he stretched out his hand to her.

Dym shyly shook her head.

"No, only I am so glad to be able to do anything for you, and—and it seems so strange looking back at those old days, Mr. Chichester."

"Mr. Chichester! you must find some better name than that, it sounds cold from my little friend's lips. How your hand trembles! There, God bless you, my—my child!"

He bit his lip as though he had suddenly remembered something, and Dym drew back into the shadow of the curtain, strangely agitated and happy.

Yes happy! though once she had been his betrothed wife, and now things were at an end between them, and he was only her friend.

Dym's simplicity and unselfishness stood her in good stead at this juncture of her life; she had accepted a difficult position with the grace and unconsciousness of a child. She had met her lover that first day with some natural agitation, but the sight of his suffering had banished all feeling of weakness into the background; he was ill and needed her, that was sufficient for the present, the future must take care of itself. When her work was finished—ah well, she could but go away again—she must not think of herself now, and so she moved about his room with a face of sweet gravity that moved Guy strangely with a thousand vague feelings of remorse and pity.

"You are altered, Dym," he once said to her, passing his hand softly over her hair, "you are worn and thin and look years older, and all this nursing will not bring the roses back."

"I can do without them," was the quiet answer, but she blushed crimson under that tender scrutiny; such speeches moved her from her calmness. Guy looked at her sadly for a moment, and then muttering some impatient protests against his weakness turned away with a sigh.

Those weeks were teaching Guy Chichester strange lessons; chained down by impatience of weakness, and brought face to face with acute suffering, what marvel if the man read the story of his life again under new lights, and weighing himself in sterner balance found himself wanting!

Life had come to him in all its reality and he had made it a pitiable failure—he had centred his all on an earthly shrine—and Divine jealousy —righteous in its retribution, unerring in its wisdom—had riven his idol from him and left him alone, maddened with his loss.

How many talents had he had entrusted to him—strength, and wealth, and intellect; philanthropy wide enough to embrace a world—influence that none could resist; and how miserably he had squandered them all! He had had his portion of goods, and no spendthrift could have wasted them more unprofitably. Great souls have great repentances; verily, there is hope, and to spare, when such men as Guy Chichester turn their faces to the wall to commune with their God and be still.

Sometimes in the dead of night when the shadows of the night-light glimmered on the ceiling, and Humphrey dozed beside, half forgotten snatches of verses that Honor used to sing came to his mind; and one especially haunted him that she had sung that Sunday night at Mentone before her baby was born.

> "While we do our duty,
>   Struggling through the tide:
> Whisper thou of beauty
>   On the other side."

"Oh, Honor, be my guardian angel still," he whispered, and out of the darkness her sweet, serene face seemed to smile on him in answer.

"He will come back, my girl, I know him well, these noble souls are not kept to wander in outer darkness. Ah! what if in the mysterious communion of saints wives in paradise do verily and indeed watch over their husbands upon earth!"

It was weeks before Guy Chichester shook off the effects of his accident, weeks before he could be moved from his bed to the couch; weeks before, a mere shadow of himself, he crept, supported by Humphrey's strong arm, to bask for an hour on the sunny terrace.

Dym looked sadly after him, as she thought of the strong, vigorous Guy Chichester of old, and contrasted him with the tall shrunken figure before her, bowed with weakness and prematurely grey-haired.

It would be long before he would look himself, she thought. The injured arm had healed, but the shock to the nervous system had been great. When the cold weather set in, he must go to the South, Dr. Grey told them; for months to come he would require care and nursing—months before he would be comparatively strong again.

Dym listened and sighed; her work was not over yet, she thought; and then she wondered what grave consultation had detained Dr. Grey so long in the library that morning. Mr. Chichester had been more than usually thoughtful for some days, and Dym was sure something was on his mind; he had scarcely looked at her or spoken to her lately; and yet, when he had addressed her, his manner had been as kind as usual.

It was October now, and the evenings were growing chilly; a small wood fire of Guy's favourite pine knots had been lighted in the library, and Guy, who was weary with his unusual exertion, had been lying quietly all the afternoon—half dozing, half enjoying the pleasant warmth—when he suddenly roused into a sitting posture and asked for Dym.

"She is here," in a quiet voice behind him. "I thought you were asleep, and was afraid to disturb you even for this," showing the glass in her hand.

"Always my attentive nurse," looking at her gratefully and drinking the restorative. "You are pale and tired, Dym; I shall have to be waiting on you next."

She smiled at that—a quaint little smile—but full of sweetness.

"I shall have time to rest when you have dismissed your nurse, Mr. Chichester."

"Mr. Chichester—always Mr. Chichester!—so you are waiting for your dismissal, eh?"

His tone was so abrupt, almost displeased, that Dym looked in his face quite startled; what she saw there made her flush scarlet.

"Come, and sit down, you are right; I am growing tired of my nurse, I want my little companion instead. Nay," as she faltered out some excuse about leaving him, "I have long been thinking we ought to have some talk together, you and I."

"By-and-bye, another time—not to-night," stammered Dym. She was trembling from head to foot. "Why did he want to speak to her? he was well now, and she must tell him that she must go away again."

"Poor child, she has grown to be afraid of me," he said gently smoothing her hair and drawing her closer to him. "Dym, have you ceased to trust your friend?"

Her only answer was to hide her face in her hands, and pray him to spare her. Bursting into tears she implored him not to speak to her—to let her go—and not be good to her, for she could not bear it.

"Why should I let you go when I want you?" he answered gently, and there was something in his firm pressure of her hands that soothed even her exceeding agitation. "Dym, I never mean to let you go—what do you mean, have you forgotten your promise?"

"What promise?"

"To stay with me while I wanted you. Dym, I want you always. Did you not understand my meaning; I was too weak to explain."

"No, no," she said, starting from him. "Mr. Chichester, you must not talk so; it is not right when you know——" she stopped, and her face was dyed with crimson.

"What do I know, dear? that you are my affianced wife?"

"No, no," she repeated in a heart-broken tone. "We have altered that—my letter has altered that. No, do not be kind to me," as he only pressed her hand more tenderly. "I have given you back your troth; you are free, quite free, I have made you so. I am nothing to you —nothing but the poor little friend who has loved and nursed you."

He smiled at that a sweet benign smile that seemed to bless her, and strove to draw her more into his sheltering arm.

"I think you are more than my little friend."

"No, Guy, I am not," using his name for the first time in her agitation.

"Yes, you are; you are my darling, my wife that is to be. I have never been free, I never wish to be free. Have you misunderstood me all this time, my child? It has come to this, that I cannot do without you, Dym, that I want you always."

Did she dream the words, or did he speak them? was that earnest voice, so sad and yet so sweet, speaking to her?

"I have my faults, no man more; but I never wilfully deceived you; I have buried the best part of my life in Honor's grave; nay, do not shrink from me, dear, I have told you this before; if you can be content with such love as I can give you, for God's sake come to me, Dym, and make my desolate life less desolate. I love you very dearly for your own sweet sake."

"Really and truly, Guy?"

"Really and truly, sweetheart."

"Oh, I am happy!" Dym scarcely breathed the words, but Guy heard them, and with a strength of which he could scarcely believe himself capable, he lifted the little creature in his arms, and felt her nestle to his bosom, keeping her there till she had sobbed out her artless confession of love and sorrow.

"You must teach me to be more worthy of it, Dym, darling," he said gravely, when their excitement had a little subsided, and Dym sat beside him with her dark eyes brilliant with shy happiness. "I have been a sad failure; what am I that two such pure hearts should have made me their happiness?" and a look of terrible exhaustion passed over his face as he recalled his wasted life.

"You must not talk any more, Guy," she whispered, laying her little hand timidly on his forehead. Guy paid it tribute gratefully as it passed his lips. "You must let me be your nurse a little longer without wearying of her."

"You shall be what you like," he replied, unclosing his eyes; "but I know what I shall soon want to make you."

Dym's head drooped against his arm, but she made no answer.

And so the last cobwebs were swept away, and the great dazzled sun of requited love shone down into Dymphna Elliott's woman-kingdom; the evil fairy had done her work and earned her own confusion.

Guy Chichester was not one to brook long delays; Dym had suffered enough, and he wanted her sweet ministries in all their entirety. "When will you come to your grey-haired lover?" he said one day smiling fondly as she took her low seat beside him, and looked up at him with worshipping eyes. "Little Sunbeam, I want you always shining on me; you have no idea how dark it is when you are away."

"What do you mean, Guy?" but she knew what he meant, and blushed beautifully. And Guy, who loved beauty in women, and remembered Honor's perfect grace, thought, with a strange thrill of pleasure, how very pretty Dym had grown, and wondered that he had never noticed it before.

And so it was, that one gusty November day, in a strange old city church, Dymphna Elliott became Guy Chichester's wife. Humphrey gave her away, honest Humphrey, who craved to do it, with the tears in his eyes. Humphrey, who took her in his arms and blessed her, and put her hand in Guy's.

"I doubt if even you are worthy of her, Squire," he said gruffly; "but the gift of such a heart must make any man rich. There, good-bye, God bless you, dear, and don't forget your old friend Humphrey."

Forget him! Does a woman ever forget the man who has blessed her with his honest love? Dym ever clave to Humphrey with truest, deepest affection, when out of the wealth and glory of her perfected life she strove that a little sunshine should stream on the path of the childless man; when his dream had come true, and her children and Guy's climbed upon his knees, and filled his lonely home with childish voices, when she could smile on him and call him friend and brother, and knew his honest heart felt no pang, and only rejoiced in her happiness.

And who could measure that happiness?

Look at her sweet face, which her husband declares grows sweeter every day, and which no cloud of regret ever darkens; is there any limit to her joy?

Day by day she knows she is more surely winning the noble heart of Guy Chichester; day by day he looks at her with fuller content, with deeper tenderness; day by day the deadly wound of his lost love heals into chastened remembrance and present peace.

"My wife has been my comforter," he said once to Humphrey, and Humphrey looked at him with his old wistful smile and nodded, and

Guy went back across the ploughed wintry fields, and under the starlight, and saw the light of home shining through the leafless trees.

"You are late, love; little Humphrey has been waiting to say 'Good-night' to you;" a little figure in shining silk glides out of the firelight and steals into his arms.

"Were you waiting for me, my wife? I was with Humphrey—nay, never mind our boy; we have been talking of you, Sweetheart."

"Of me!" She lifts her loving eyes in surprise as he holds her closely, very closely, to him, and then releases her.

"What, wondering, love! Nay, I was only telling Humphrey that my little wife has been my comforter."

THE END.

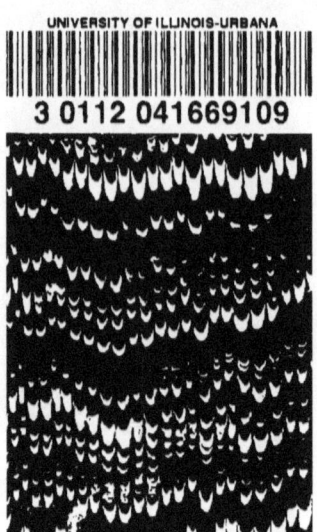

www.ingramcontent.com/pod-product-compliance
Lightning Source LLC
Chambersburg PA
CBHW031350230426
43670CB00006B/488